Sailing without Ahab

Ecopoetic Travels

Steve Mentz

Fordham University Press   New York   2024

Sailing without Ahab

for my parents,
Marilyn and Roger Mentz

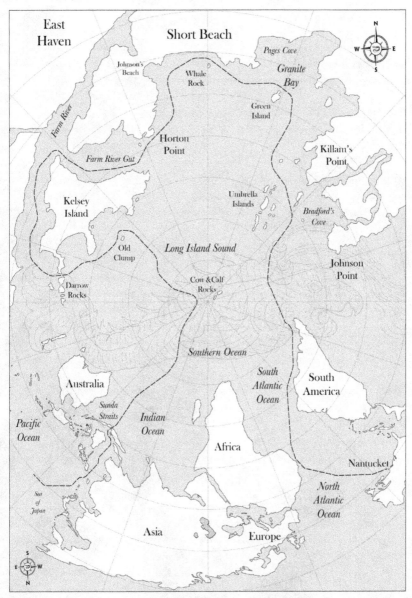

Map created by John Wyatt Greenlee of Surprised Eel Mapping.

Contents

Foreword

by Suzanne Conklin Akbari

> But when that smoking chowder came in, the
> mystery was delightfully explained. Oh, sweet
> friends! hearken to me. It was made of small juicy
> clams, scarcely bigger than hazel nuts, mixed
> with pounded ship biscuit, and salted pork cut up
> into little flakes; the whole enriched with butter,
> and plentifully seasoned with pepper and salt.
>
> (*Moby-Dick*, ch. 15, "Chowder")

This is a book about subtraction. Ahab and all that he brings with
him—patriarchal authority; colonial violence; the monomania
of capitalism—are imaginatively subtracted from the narrative
arc of Melville's novel. What we find instead is a rendering of
Moby-Dick that luxuriates in the watery depths and the foamy
shallows, experiencing the aquatic world not from the vantage
point of shipboard but on the wet sand and stones of the Con-
necticut shore. This book thus sits as an imaginative contribution
to the body of work in the blue humanities that Steve Mentz is
known for, drawing on ecocritical scholarship to imagine other
ways of being in the world, and possible paths to remediating the
damages to nature that humanity has wrought.[1]

Or, maybe, this is a book about sublimation. *Sailing without
Ahab* is a rendering of Melville's *Moby-Dick*: rendered, that is,
boiled down from the fatty flesh of the whale, melting into a trans-
parent and pure oil. This melting transforms not only the flesh of
the whale but also the flesh of the men aboard ship, as they squeeze
one another's hands through the spermaceti. As Melville puts
it, "Come; let us squeeze hands all round; nay, let us all squeeze

Figure 1. Courtney Leonard, "Contact, 2021" [detail]

ourselves into each other; let us squeeze ourselves universally into the very milk and sperm of kindness" (ch. 94, "A Squeeze of the Hand").² Here, the sublime is achieved through the interpenetration of enfleshed bodies, hand in hand, grasping one another through the pure matter of the whale's body—not completely liquid and not solid. A state of being in-between, being together.

The body is at the center of sublime experience in *Sailing without Ahab* as well. But instead of oil, the slippery medium is the sea; and instead of intimate congress, we remain in the realm of the individual subject—sometimes reaching back in time to grasp a half-forgotten memory, sometimes reaching forward speculatively toward shorelines that are only just becoming visible. This is a solitary voyage but one that holds the promise of future connections. These are mediated through the double self of the narrator of *Sailing without Ahab*, the "I." who is at once Melville's narrator (in an abbreviation of "Ishmael") and the "I" or self who narrates the present work. They sit together in an uneasy apposition, united in their revulsion at the tyrannical Ahab and all he represents and divided in their very different ways of relating to others—especially to "I.".'s beloved "Q."

Or, maybe, this is a book about subjection. To be a subject is, in part, to be subjected—to the command of others (Ahab!), to the requirements of the political and economic systems we inhabit, to the desires and passions of the body. This formation of the subject takes place, in Melville's *Moby-Dick*, both directly, by means of Ishmael's experience (of melancholy, of tyranny, of affectionate love, etc.), and indirectly, as the looming presence of the white whale throws into relief all those who stand in its shadow. In *Sailing without Ahab*, the formation of the subject takes place incrementally, with each individual portion of the narrative—poem, prose piece, discursive note—adding up to a great counterweight to Melville's novel, sailing near to it at moments with close textual correspondences and deviating from its course at others. Just as the individual chapters and headnotes of *Moby-Dick* add up into a capacious, even encyclopedic account of the world, so the individual poems and framing prose pieces of *Sailing without Ahab* add up to an account of the swimmer's world—in other words, a microcosm of the great globe traversed by the white whale, centered on Mentz's own home beach in Connecticut with its Whale Rock.

Sailing without Ahab navigates its relationship to *Moby-Dick* in three distinct ways: folio, quarto, and octavo. Or, to put it another way: it matches poems and chapters, in a sequence of pairs; it inserts additional poems that correspond conceptually, rather than formally, to elements in Melville's novel; and it frames itself between two prose punctuations, a Headless Travels introduction and a Critical Postscript, that explicate or elaborate on the larger frameworks that undergird the book, especially the project of the blue humanities. Each of these elaborates the relationship of novel and compilation in its own distinctive way. Some poems, such as "The Pulpit," "Chowder," and "The Mast-Head" (plus many more), bear the titles of chapters of *Moby-Dick*. These are in a particularly intimate intertextual relationship with the novel: each encounter is, so to speak, a two-page folio spread where the reader sees Melville's chapter on the left page and Mentz's answering poem on the right. Other poems, such as "Out of Place" or "A Bosom Friend," filter the nineteenth-century novel through the individual experience of the twenty-first-century self. Here, solitary embodiment—embraced by the sea, bathed in light, shrouded in darkness—is at the fore, at times producing an encyclopedic excess that manifests itself in the form of the list.[3] See, for example, the tripping listiness of the opening lines of "A Bosom Friend":

No place like a bed and no love like Q.
No warmth like the sun and no ship like the P.
No food like chowder and no book like his tattoos.

Finally, the framing prose sections punctuate the stream of lyric poems, intervening in a different voice to gesture outside the bounds of *Sailing without Ahab*, pointing toward other ships and other voyages that nonetheless traverse the same ocean.

Sometimes these gestures lead to other books and even other textual traditions that respond to *Moby-Dick*. For example, Mentz makes note of Richard J. King's *Ahab's Rolling Sea: A Natural History of Moby-Dick*, which uses the novel to ground a wide-ranging exploration of the natural world, its past, and its possible futures.[4] He also mentions C. L. R. James's engagement with Melville's novel in his *Mariners, Renegades and Castaways: The Story of Herman Melville and the World We Live In*, published in 1953 in the wake of James's confinement at Ellis Island and, ultimately, deportation to England.[5] I can do no more than scratch the surface of the rich intertextual relationship of Melville's novel and James's manifesto, much less their shared reflection in *Sailing without Ahab*; but it is worth noting just one point of contact. The subtitle of James's book reveals the temporal commitments of his project, juxtaposing the congregation of sailors aboard the *Pequod* with the assemblage of those passing through New York Harbor under the shadow of Lady Liberty:

> The whole of the world is represented on Ellis Island. Many sailors, but not only sailors; Germans, Italians, Latvians, Swedes, Filipinos, Malays, Chinese, Hindus, Pakistanis, West Indians, Englishmen, Australians, Danes, Yugoslavs, Greeks, Canadians, representatives of every Latin-American country. As I write each word, I see someone

whom I knew. To the administration on Ellis Island . . . , these are just a body of isolated individuals who are in reality seeking charity, or a home in the United States which is a better place to live in than their backward or poverty-stricken countries. Of all the blunders I encountered on Ellis Island this is undoubtedly the most colossal. These men, taken as a whole, know the contemporary world and know it better than many world-famous foreign correspondents.[6]

James is acknowledging and responding to the heterogeneous crew of the *Pequod*, gathered from the four corners of the earth. And we see them here too, refracted through the poetic lens of *Sailing without Ahab*:

First come two Nantucket Sailors, but the rest are called out by
    nations and places:
Dutch Sailor, French Sailor, Iceland Sailor, Maltese Sailor, Sicilian
    Sailor,
Long-Island Sailor, Azores Sailor, China Sailor, Lascar Sailor,
Sicilian Sailor, Tahitian Sailor, Portuguese Sailor, Danish Sailor,
English Sailor, Old Manx Sailor, St. Jago's Sailor, Spanish Sailor,
    Belfast Sailor.
Sprinkled among them a few names:
Pip, Tashtego, Daggoo. The voices intermingle
With echoing songs and contrasting colors.
("Forecastle—Midnight")

Such passages—whether in Melville's nineteenth-century novel, James's twentieth-century manifesto, or Mentz's twenty-first-century lyric compilation—at once emphasize both multiplicity and singularity. The multiplicity of humankind is refracted visually in "contrasting colors" and audibly in "echoing songs," while their diverse places of origin are preserved in the exuberant list of places: "Germans, Italians, Latvians, Swedes, Filipinos, Malays, Chinese, Hindus, Pakistanis, West Indians, Englishmen, Australians, Danes, Yugoslavs, Greeks, Canadians . . . " The singularity of humankind, by contrast, appears in moments of transcendence, whether the squeezing of hands in a vat of spermaceti or the embrace of the solitary swimmer's body in the waters of Long Island Sound.

This dance of multiplicity and singularity, extended over almost two centuries, is brought into the present moment with the artwork "Contact, 2021" by Courtney M. Leonard, pictured both above (in a close-up detail) and below (in full view). Leonard's work, which can be seen as part of the Offshore Art movement, explores the relationships of land, water, oceanic life, and regional history from a specifically Shinnecock perspective.[7] Made of individually shaped, painted, and glazed ceramic "shells," sewn with artificial sinew onto a canvas pierced with brass fittings, this artwork inhabits the littoral space between the natural and artificial worlds. It also brings together land and water: looking at this monumental artwork—6 feet by 6 feet—from a distance reveals that it is also a map, showing the political entity of the state of New York, limned by the waterways that border the state—ocean to the south and east and penetrated by the rivers that flow within. Glazed in white and purple, the ceramic "shells" evoke the wampum that continues to be handcrafted and used in ceremony by Shinnecock people today.

This artwork is a political map in two ways: it depicts both the state of New York, reflecting the settler colony that predates the emergence of the United States as a nation, and the political entity of the Shinnecock people, whose traditional homeland is on what is now called "Long Island" but which historically was defined by the waterways that the people traveled and the relationships they formed throughout that oceanic region.

Like the individual chapters of Melville's novel, like the lyric fragments of *Sailing without Ahab*, Courtney Leonard's "Contact, 2021" inhabits a particular historical moment while also extending backward into historical time, and forward into potential futures. Each "shell" is exquisitely detailed, each one with its own story, united into a seamless whole. We see, for example:

a bridge
two towers
a three-masted sailing vessel
a deer, or stag
a windmill
Liberty's torch

FIGURE 2. Courtney Leonard, "Contact, 2021"

Like the individual persons representing the "whole of the world" (in C. L. R. James's words) who pass through Ellis Island, the ceramic "shells" of Courtney Leonard's "Contact, 2021" maintain their individuality while also participating in larger patterns. Yet Leonard's work is profoundly different from both Melville and James in that her work is grounded in Indigenous political identity, specifically, in Shinnecock identity. Place, homeland, and home waters appear differently depending on the vantage point of the one who sees—whether from the Mast-Head or from the edge of the sea. From the vantage point of Leonard's "Contact, 2021," we hear the voices of Queequeg, and of those people who are remembered in the name of the *Pequod*, in a different register.[8]

Notes

1. Steve Mentz, *An Introduction to the Blue Humanities* (Abingdon: Routledge, 2024). A conversation about the blue humanities appears in Nathen R. Strohmeyer. "Our Blue Future: A Conversation with Steve Mentz, *Los Angeles Review of Books*, 3 October 2020, *https://lareviewofbooks.org/article/our-blue-future-a-conversation-with-steve-mentz/*.

2. Melville, *Moby-Dick*, 323. A conversation about the slippery togetherness of this passage can be found in Episode 12: *Moby-Dick* (4 July 2019) of Chris Piuma and Suzanne Conklin Akbari, *The Spouter-Inn; or, a Conversation with Great Books*, *https://www.megaphonic.fm/spouter/12*.

3. On the encyclopedism of Melville's *Moby-Dick* and the *De proprietatibus rerum* of Bartholomaeus Anglicus, see Suzanne Conklin Akbari, "The Encyclopedic Genius of Melville's Masterpiece: On *Moby-Dick* as a Way of Seeing the World," *Literary Hub*, 1 August 2019, https://lithub.com/the-encyclopedic-genius-of-melvilles-masterpiece/. On the genre of the list, see Eva von Contzen and James Simpson, eds., *Enlistment: Lists in Medieval and Early Modern Literature* (Columbus: Ohio State University Press, 2022).

4. Richard J. King, *Ahab's Rolling Sea: A Natural History of "Moby-Dick"* (Chicago: University of Chicago Press, 2019).

5. C. L. R. James, *Mariners, Renegades and Castaways: The Story of Herman Melville and the World We Live In* (Hanover, NH: University Press of New England, [1953] 1978).

6. James, *Mariners*, 151–52.

7. The Offshore Art movement emerged explicitly through the *Radical Seafaring* exhibition curated by Andrea Grover at the Parrish Art Museum, Water Mill, New York, 8 May–24 July 2016. See the exhibition catalog, *Radical Seafaring*, by Andrea Grover, with contributions by Sasha Archibald, Alexander Dumbadze, Christopher French, Dylan Gauthier, Andrea Grover, and Terrie Sultan (Water Mill, NY: Parrish Art Museum, 2016; distributed by DelMonico Books / Prestel). See also Pei-Ru Keh, "To the High Seas: Parrish Art Museum Devotes Its Latest Show to 'Offshore Art,'" *Wallpaper** 2016 (updated 2 July 2022), *https://www.wallpaper.com/art/parrish-art-museum-devotes-its-latest-show-radical-seafaring-to-offshore-art*.

8. For a provocative reading of Melville's Queequeg—especially the tattoos on his body and the "hieroglyphics" on his coffin—in the context of Indigenous writing technologies, see Birgit Brander Rasmussen, *Queequeg's Coffin: Indigenous Literatures and Early American Literature* (Durham, NC: Duke University Press, 2022), 111–38.

Sailing without Ahab

Etymology (Supplied by
a late consumptive Professor)

We know the words,
All except one.

Poems carry bodies out to sea
Because we're all looking for something—
For light, or the means to make it.

Our voyage plows one hundred thirty-eight swells,
One for each chapter, plus the Etymology, Extracts, and
      Epilogue.
Only one word's forbidden,
Only one wooden leg left onshore.

What's our way, without his madness?
What orders remain once we have cast away
The Captain's law?

Hval or *Whale, Baleine* or *Ballena.*
Our big body, our shared goal,
Object,
Flashing flukes-high in Pacific light.

I. wants the biggest place.

With Jonah we enter flesh,
Past scrimshaw walls,
Down monstrous throat.
Unhingedness vacuums flesh
Into depth.

Down's our direction.
Rolling and wallowing past

The circle of jaws
To settle inside rib-arches,
Still and contained.

Bodies descend.
Water squeezes thick and heavy
Around that greater body, our bodies,
All bodies.
All the world's wet film covering.
We feel
Depth as embrace,
Ocean as possibility,
Lightlessness as bosom.

We don't know why the prophet resurfaced.
But sailing headless means
Seeking after something new.

So much that we love floats before us—
But not him.

Sailing Without

We left without him.
It was snowing. The next day was a holiday
We thought better to encounter offshore.

No one thought much about him
As we sailed out to sea.

I'm not going to tell you it wasn't confusing
To sail headless into chaos
And never to feel that burning drive
Or the pegleg's tapping rhythm
On the wooden deck.

In the end I. thinks only Pip missed the Captain.
The Quaker mate drank coffee.
Stubb chewed his pipe.
Flask wagged.

Tashtego's eyes swiveled so'west toward Gay Head.
Daggoo glared out to sea.
And Q. spied the unmapped true place.

But I. alone—
        All alone—
Forgets to tell the tale.

Headless Travels

Close your eyes. Smell the sea. Feel the deck settle and sway under your feet. Let fluid pull the mass of your body. Unthinkable creatures swim beneath you. Labyrinthine waters beckon. The air tastes salt. There's a book over your shoulder, but you can't quite see it.

We're not taking the same trip, though we sail in the same direction. This time, the *P.*'s American voyage steers across the curvature of the World Ocean without anyone at the helm. The ship overflows with plurality—multiracial, visionary, queer, conflicted, polyphonic, playful, violent. But today something is different. We sail headless without any domineering Captain. Instead of binding ourselves to dismasted rage, the ship's crew seeks only what we will find: currents teeming with life, a blue-watered alien globe, toothy cetacean smiles from vasty deeps. Treasures await those who sail without.

These poems, full of swimming and reading, balanced atop books and coastal rocks, encountering whales and literary phantoms, launch into oceanic chaos without the stabilizing focus of a Nantucket captain. Guided by waywardness and curiosity, these verses seek an alien ecopoetics of marine depths, a refraction of light, the taste of salt on skin. Directionless, we reach down into the water. It's not an easy voyage, and not a certain one. It lures you forward. It has fixed its barbed hook in me.

Order isn't our guiding principle. The poems have a fixed total but don't individually have numbers. They follow the voyage but don't bind you to its mast. Read in whatever order you like. Let your eyes swim back to front, waywardly, in small clusters or arbitrary dips. Follow my titles or Herman's. Let the pages fall open of their own devices. Sailing without opens bodies to randomness and movement.

A Book Over Your Shoulder

We sail with a familiar crew. You will recognize Starbuck, Stubb, Flask. No longer intimidated by the dismasted tyrant who's not on board, the mates show themselves as fakers, posing with authority, supporting structures that never appear. Q.'s on the voyage too, his tattooed body lovingly spied by pensive I. High above, perched and dangerously drowsy on the masthead, I. stares at Q., views Pip's descent, Fedallah's gloom, the blaze of Perth's forge, the Old Manxman chanting prophecies. Everyone is here, except one.

Ecopoetic travels plough wayward pathways. There's much to confuse but also much that will be familiar to readers of that *draught of a draught*, our unfinishable sacred text of oceanic longing. Leaving the Captain on shore means leaving Herman behind too, but even lacking authority and author much remains. The book beckons, just out of sight. This voyage craves new things to love.

We seek the same blubber-encased prey and gam with the same whaleships. To *sail without* means not to venture to new places but to see the wonder-world in expanses and deeps. We hunt new possibilities in old waters. In places the Captain's electric outline appears in ghostly negative, showing in the text with square brackets. "[. . .]" is not our Captain. It's fine to notice, to remember him, to recall his sonorous authority. But we're not under his command this time.

The voyage surges in currents. Each poem flows into, intermingles with, sloshes through and against the others. Like water in water, each stream enmeshes each other one. Sometimes it's hard to know just where we are swimming.

The biggest fish after which I. hurls my spear-poems is a scheme for oceanic living in the Anthropocene. This book hunts through poetry, immersion, and imagination for ways to keep afloat in rising and stormy seas. Climate change and sea level rise mean, among other things, that the world's oceans are encroaching on dry land. Living near the sea means living with a flood that will not subside. These poems seize upon the skeleton of American literature's most determined effort to capture the sea in words. I. aims to swim with the whaleship, drowse at the masthead, hurl harpoons with Q., sound deeply with the White Whale. Oceanic truths surface, though not to be struck. Sailing headless means accommodating uncertainties. These poems sketch an unfinished plan for our oceanic Anthropocene.

There is no master on this ship. While the one-legged Captain remains Herman's most iconic human figure, his visible symbol, his horrifying lure, we leave the bad man home. In abandoning dominion and rage, we escape suffering and electric charge. We still hunt whales—even, in the end, the White Whale—but no one drives our seeking. So many horrors flow from just one man's violence: the tunnel-vision quest, the God-killing meditations, the colonial doubloon nailed into the mast. With no Captain, the ship's plurality opens all the way. Whales still pay the ultimate price even on such a haphazard hunt. Sailors and officers hurl themselves into crooked jaws. But released into freedom, the ship seeks entanglements. We find other species. We glimpse different futures.

We resist tyranny through absence. Without his name, his presence, his command, new things become possible. New knowledges emerge from vacancy. We're not the first to have seen the wonder-world. But we hope, through the refraction of lyric, to spy different things.

Replacing the Captain's centrality with the bow-oarsman's waywardness generates a variable expansion of "I.," an autobiographical presence who spans a nineteenth-century fictional whaleman and my own embodied twenty-first-century self. I. sleeps at the mast-head and plies a bow oar in search of whales. I. walks my dogs and swims in the silty saltwater of Long Island Sound. This book's map draws these two places together. To splash through the *P*.'s oceans and my local waters interleaves a literary past with an elastic present. I. lives in the Anthropocene. To live ecologically in these circumstances requires new ways to love our nonhuman world.

These poems love Q. more than cetaceans of any color. No longer distracted by the old man's fixation, space unfurls for I.'s desiring gaze. The mystical marriage between cranky schoolteacher and open-armed South Sea islander imagines an erotic and companionate ideal. The garrulous narrator and pidgin-speaking cannibal present ecological and human opposites. They arrive on the whaleship from different sides of the World Ocean. My vision, like Herman's, shows their love entwining itself around and in opposition to the blood lust of the hunt. The queer tragic love story becomes a path toward ecological survival—or partial survival. This isn't a new idea. But shifting the Captain out of the way enables a different experience. We embark onto Anthropocene seas seeking freedom, risk, and possibility.

Many know that we've been on a polyvocal voyage all along. Not even the living Captain, with his singularity and his oratory, ever silenced the voices of ship or deep. The tale has created many twists and turns, from C. L. R. James's indictment of tyranny to early Cold War fantasies about individualism to post-human eco-materialist recuperations of the mad Captain. All these sea stories are true, and looked at from a certain angle, these poems swim alongside current trends in eco-theoretical literary criticism. But the poems don't only cleave those waters. Readers who are Melville scholars may want to start with the Critical Postscript, which connects this project to the dual contexts of Melville studies and ecomaterialist theory. The postscript performs a scholarly reintegration of the more fugitive impulses of these poems. But if you are here for the poems first, it's worth reading the poems first.

To unfurl a headless voyage in verse reanimates the *P*.'s doomed hunt. These poems comprise creative-critical hybrids that capture in words the dizzying experience of living with and inside a canonical literary novel. In some cases the poems parallel insights that scholars limn in denser prose. But I. also follows more circuitous routes. To embark on this voyage means mixing Melville's narrator with an embodied author who lives, writes, and swims in the northeastern United States in the early twenty-first century. The poems take shape inside echoes impressed on I.'s body. Sometimes these verses approach, tangent-like, insights I. finds in scholarship. Other moments capture more tactile sensations, the feel of water on flesh, the unsettling double lives that arise in acts of reading, emotional tugs of the familiar and the strange. These are poems about immersion, about thinking, and about reading again a story that has long since gotten under I.'s skin.

My core gambit hazards that poetry revitalizes reading. For scholars and teachers, students and writers, reading comprises our most fundamental and most mysterious shared labor. I. versifies a hyper-close re-reading of *Moby-Dick*. These poems advance the art of reading through poetic co-creation. Many readers in the early twenty-first century, very much including I., live with our imaginations saturated by fast-running internal dialogues. We hear dead voices every day. These poems surface that literary haunting and make new art from it. They model a fully immersive engagement with a literary work.

The Kind of Person I. Is

I. has for a long time been the kind of person who walks through the world with lines from *Moby-Dick* ringing in my imagination. I. devoured Melville's epic for the first of many times as a melancholy teenager in New Jersey in the 1970s. I. reads and teaches and listens to and presses the book on students, neighbors, and family. For me, as for many, the story of the *P.* tells a prophetic, intimate text. These poems invite readers to walk with me and with I., distracted and speculative, sleepy and anxious, high atop the masthead or on a rocky comma of Connecticut beach. Our path is long worn, grooved into clarity by a titanic imagination. Rewandering that path with no Captain and open eyes may discern new orders, new responses to disorder, and different answers to the claims the inhuman world makes on our flesh.

Currents surface during a long voyage. Sometimes they dive deep to flow unseen. Each poem touches, sometimes tangentially, the magic pathways of the novel. I. hopes that readers who sail with me and with I., who refuse the Captain to pad down the pavement to a rocky beach at dawn, will emerge with a sense of how oceanic engagement, watery speculation, and blue thinking can invigorate minds, bodies, and imaginations. I. hopes strategies for survival and endurance during uncertain times emerge from this rewriting of an overfamiliar and intensely beloved text. Our Anthropocene challenge is to learn to live with the inhuman, through each orange sunrise glow, globe-transfiguring pandemic, and unseasonable flood. These poems aim to make our living less orderly, more pleasurable, and imaginatively unsettling.

We sail better on the voyage with no Captain.

No Order No Story No Ending

Here's the way I. plays the game. I. opens my book at random, reads, turns the pages. Sometimes I. splashes straight ahead, two, three, six poems in a row. Sometimes I. flips forward twenty pages, or sometimes back thirty. Every page might open a new turning, a new sorting. There's no order, which means no story, which means no ending. Whales are out there, but I. is not heading straight for them.

It's not the usual reader's quest, but it's an ancient practice, the *sortes virgilianae*, recently digitized by the glorious lamented twitterbot @MobyDickatSea. There's always a sacred book to show the way forward. Page numbers need not constrain you. We aren't seeking anything. The White Whale swims, dives, feeds. But he's not all we're after.

There's urgency and violence in the dominion of story. I. wants to sail another way. When I. feels the desire to cast my lance at Great White Evil God, when thick blood becomes I.'s only measure—then, we can't sail fast enough. We hail each stranger captain: "Hast seen the White Whale?" We steer toward his own particular waters. But that's not the only way this voyage turns.

Without [. . .] all that force dissipates. Free!

How does it feel to wander with I., aimless, sleepy, philosophical? To trace sideways across these pages, to turn for any reason or none, to move by I.'s own not-understood rhythms?

It's hard to know how to end. I. grants you that.

Loomings

Listen!
The rain knows
what's coming.
Tiny fingers you can't feel because
     with the slightest human touch they
dissolve
Splash-tapping
On my window, now, just now,
Tonight
Tear-shapes command—

There's no escape from hypos but hydration:
In! In!
I. must go into it, onto it, out beyond
to where
Is nothing but blue-green,
Wonder-worlds
teeming
phantoms
Awash with life.

Come ship with me—
Follow I.—
Less orderly
More desperate
Unmapped.

If you don't follow you can't see.

Out of Place

There's a whale in Labrador Pond.

It's too big.
In a freshwater pond only about a half-mile wide,
Each edge rounded off by lily pads and marsh,
Fed by a trickle through a rusty under-dirt-road culvert,
There's no place for a whale.
He came here with me.
I. finds no place else for him.
So in he splashes, fin-full and overflowing,
Displacing with massive girth
Water that surges onto the porch to soak my feet where I. sits
With my family playing Clue.
It's hard to know who did it.
The whale's swimming stirs up green froth.
Its body rips algae-fronds from the silty bottom.
Air bubbles ascend, balloon, and pop.
In the morning I. wakes to devastation.

I. brews coffee and hot chocolate and bakes biscuits while
    sleepers dream
Of a bigger place.

Fishing

Some things remain hard to see.
Like a great fish below the surface
hooked
And straining whirling water with hidden tail.

I. sits in a boat with my father, staring
At something neither of us can make out.

Fish-hooks curl question marks,
Barbing themselves in cold flesh,
Flashing into the sky with a flick of paternal wrist
Or the overhand spiral I. learned as a child,
Taught to my own son,
And that I. interrogatingly casts out today.

A man can be honest in any sort of skin, sez I.
But a fisherman—what honesty
Sets bait to a steel hook?

What has I. learned, what is I. teaching?

Change

> . . . It's the most important question—
What does it feel like, how does it
Hit you, what happens to your body when it
> Changes
And the things you were expecting to feel you don't
> Feel
> anymore?

Some mornings I. wakes in darkness,
Steals furtively through the silent house,
Sneaks out the door,
Walks down the hill onto a comma of sand and rock.

There's haze and glow, but no fiery outline,
No blaze and orb to announce another future—
Only a blank, a pause, a moment between
Any moments that might yet come.

I. turns my back on the sea before the sun comes up.

Vision

To undivide attention isn't easy.
It narrows
Mind and body.
Presses in a sharpness that bears no questions,
A point that culminates in no interrogative hook,
So that the only thing that is, lies before you,
The only thing that matters, reflects your eyes,
The only thing that compels, squats beside you,
And the only action possible in a dark sublunary world
Is to see.

The Street

What is it like to go out?
Out your door, which opens onto another door,
Or a street, town, city, nation.

Or can we open
All the way—
            onto open-ness, into
Empty
            Virus-filled
                        Air?

The dog walks with me
To the ocean each early morning. Together we spy
Vacancy. At the end of
Eyesight I. glimpses the haze line of Long Island,
Twenty miles away.

It's not that I. wants to swim there,
Or even that I. thinks about the bodies that
            Populate that undistant shoreline,
Connected circuitously by asphalt lines.

But when I. sees sun-shimmer on the blue
Stretching across to another coast
I. craves immersion, motion, and
Wonder. Worlds.

The Chapel

I. worships on that gritty comma, between
High and low tides, smelling salt and seaweed,
Where egrets graze and gulls caw.

I. was there last night, after a thunderstorm.
High tide sluiced sand off granite, which grabbed my bare feet
As I. balanced and took two big steps, one, two,
And then—
Jumped onto cold sand.

The ebb had rolled all the way out past the seaweed,
Revealing the dirty underclothing of the world.
Green weed insinuated slime between my toes,
Which dug down into water-smoothed grit.

No sun, no stars, no moon. The egrets which feed on low tide
Mornings were nowhere to be seen.
I. could spy vagueness,
Stretching out to the dark.
I. could hear the slow lap of water moving.
Just a hint of salt burned in my nose.

The Pulpit

When I. stands on granite forced askew by glacial retreat,
And I. places bare feet on abrasive stone,
And I. looks down past the water-mark on an out-stretching
Rock from which I. dives in high-tide summers,
And I. smells seaweed salt and ripeness,
And below that sees slow-surging waters,
And if I. is lucky sometimes the white shock of an egret's
Bended neck aiming at something beneath the surface,
And high above in impossible blue the hidden osprey's call
Tells that he sees something we can't,
That he has spied fish-movement beneath sun-glare,
And he'll dive soon, passing from the sea of air to that thicker,
Greener, more viscous fluid, seeking food and knowledge and
Illumination—

Then I. preaches from my pulpit.

Storm and Wreck

Woe, says the ancient sailor,
To him who seeks to pour oil on the waters
When God has brewed them into a gale!

I. puzzles those words in the storm,
When water rages beyond confines,
Fits itself beyond containers,
Spills out to soak bodies and flood dry places.

What is *woe*? A sadness that comes from loss,
Not destruction but a sudden absence of
Order, of the way things were, patterns that can be
Explained.

What does *oil* mean to a mariner, a preacher, a
Poet? Thick warm liquid poured onto the curling locks
Of boy-kings, the whale's secret case, the black fire
With which we have flamed the planet?

How does God *brew* gales? What turnings and combinations,
What measurings and bakings,
What pauses and re-starts,
What unknowable plans does it take to create the disorder
From which we yearn to make meaning,
Raining down on us from Him?

A Bosom Friend

No place like a bed and no love like Q.
No warmth like the sun and no ship like the *P*.
No food like chowder and no book like his tattoos.
No task like head-selling and no place like New Bedford.
No shave but with a harpoon and no breakfast but beefsteaks.
No head but George Washington's and no hat but Abe's.
No kindness but pagan and no simplicity but his heart.
No chill like the darkness and no blanket but his idol.
No warmth but a low fire and no voyage but for whales.
No smoke but from his pipe and no chat but til morning.
No future but with him and no ship but the *P*.
No place like a bed and no love like Q.

Ideas

How can we know when futures hit us?

Picture: the cozy pair in bed,
Smoking a long pipe,
Chattering about nothing,
Deferring sleep.

Pale and tattooed legs cross and uncross.

Somewhere deep in ocean's darkness
An idea appears—
Births itself, rushes toward the surface, sounds,
Breaches into fullness,
And no one takes any notice.

Mapping Oceans

True places never mark maps.
Home occupies no territory.

When I. was a boy and my life was about to change
I. swam out into the froth off the Jersey shore
After a late-summer storm.
The disorganized surf echoed the three days' blow,
Tropical violence had followed the Gulf Stream
North, into the place I. was about to leave.
The water remembered the storm's power,
Confusedly, in many directions at once,
So that froth and curls pushed me one way,
Then another, before dipping over my eyes
And salt-stinging my throat.

I. went out too far.
I. knew it when I. turned to face the shore
And saw where the undertow had towed me.

It was a long, slow, arrhythmic swim back,
Each time
Trying not to lose too much distance to the backward suction
Of the wave forming behind me, and trying to gain as much as
    possible
From each sloppy breaker shouldering the way
I. wanted to go.

I. made it to shore, walked up the beach to my parents' home,
Needing a new map and new territories.

Houses in Houses

There's a thing I. wants to say about I. and Q.
I. is not sure it fits into lines.

So a different way—

- In the I.-focused voyage, Q. sits at the center.
- Q. is a center with no boundaries, no needs, no destination.
- Q. appears first, before the *P.*, the whale, or the Captain.
- Q. travels the waterworld, from Kokovoko to New Bedford to the *P.*
- Only after meeting and marrying Q. does I. travel to Nantucket and the *P.*

The wheelbarrow that Q. pushes out of the *Spouter-Inn* contains both his *canvas sack and hammock* and I.'s *poor carpet bag.* Already their belongings, their voyages, and their lives share a common vessel. The *P.* simply presents a larger coffin-wheelbarrow than the one Q. shoulders down the wharf to the Nantucket packet.

Was there ever such unconsciousness?

It's a drugged, sleeping I. that first encounters the *P.*

Nantucket

Two-thirds of this terraqueous globe belong to islanders.
Traveling offshore to the *elbow of sand, all beach, without a*
    background
Narrows the trajectories of I. and Q.
Like light they pass through the island-prism and scatter—
Ocean beckons, floats, entices.

What if Nantucket limns all islands,
All places out of sight of land,
Ships and shipwrecked souls,
All the hidden delights that dip
Below horizon's haze,
Invisible, not-quite-unreachable,
Ports of call on voyages to and through and past,
Surrounded by coral teeth and music,
Pearls sparkling up from fathom depths
That smile, and open, and welcome
Even the most knowing
Of travelers.

Chowder

Before any adventure it's important to eat well.

What's in the *Try-Pots*?

Clam: which is to say, something hidden, closed tight.
Cod: which means, flesh that was not long since
At the bottom of the sea.

Both, is the right answer.
Plus a pair of smoked herring
By way of variety.

Who's on the Ship?

Consisting of a short list of collectives that the *P.* contains

- Quaker whalers
- Men
- Whalemen
- I.
- Q.
- Three harpooners
- Those who will collect at least the 777th lay
- Bow oarsmen
- Knights
- Squires
- Boys from Connecticut who will not go to Alabama
- Gay Headers
- Nantucketers
- Pacific Men
- The United States of America

And a shorter list of larger collectives that the *P.* does not contain

- Whales
- White Whales
- Moby-Dick
- The World
- The Ocean

Intermittent Fasting

The preparation includes self-denial, self-abnegation, self-
Discipline. No meat,
No movement, no speech. Not for Q.,
Who sits silent behind the locked door
For a motionless day.

I. can't understand it.

For what does stillness prepare Q.?
What voyages, adventures,
Surges, tides, storms, sunsets, rain-filled dawns,
What squids and porpoises and whale-fish,
What Knights and Squires,
And what horrors, so many to sup full upon,
That starting with an empty belly
Seems no price to pay?

Sea Living

Quohog: both bivalve and hero. Both!

The one splits the water like the harpoon
    With which he shaves.
The other clings, bare vulnerable flesh,
    Enshelled on the bottom.

Would George Washington cannibalistically developed
    Eat clams?
Would bronze fingers, impossibly strong, pry open
    The shell
Squish the soft part between thumb and index,
    And hurl it past filed teeth?

When he eats the world stops.

Cannibal and mollusk build architectures
    Of ocean-living.
The one dives while the other waits.

The Prophet

Elijah knows what we don't know.
He knows where the Captain has been,
Where he sleeps (or not),
What he eats (or doesn't),
What it sounds like when Old Thunder
Cracks the sky.

He tells I. and Q. not to board the *P.*

It's not that they don't listen,
But that they don't stop.

Secrets give direction.
Who wants direction?

Tomorrow!

Leaving! Think about all that means,
Sleeplessness, anticipation, a turn of the stomach
In the middle of the night. Tomorrow!

Sometimes when I. wakes it's still dark,
And I. pads through the house in bare feet
Like it's still yesterday.
No one hears me spill black coffee
In the kitchen, no one sees me sneak outside
In the chill and glitter, a bitter brew
Stains my lips as naked toes grab smooth asphalt—
I. knows where I.'s going—
Just a few steps, around the corner, no dogs barking
And no leash in my hand, not this timeless
Time, this before-stirring astir-ness,
I. arrives at the rock I. sees every day,
The water beneath it, my neighbors' houses,
And over my left shoulder, away by east and south—
The first rose-color dreams into my eyes.

Going Aboard

In the middle of the night before the only day there is—
Today, now, now, very now—
My head ached and I. could not sleep.

Walking in darkness means hiding from the future.
I. maneuvers through dark hollows of the house,
Down stairs, through open doorways,
Around corners. I. doesn't turn on any lights.
Digital clocks wink at me
But I. doesn't look back.

Why doesn't I. want to go?
What does I. fear, in darkness and depth?

Merry Christmas

Fate leads the willing, sez Seneca,
And drags the reluctant. Both end up
On the same ship.

The *P*. sails Christmas morning,
Resplendent, dazzling, sails pregnant with wind.
I. and Q. stand at the rail, watching Nantucket
Sink. *Where do you think we're going?* mumbles I.
Kill 'em big whale fish! flashes Q.

All things born must die,
Mutters an invisible shipmate philosopher.

The Lee Shore

There's a pause at journey's end—
A still point, landfall, feet touching ground.
Voices and noises surround you.
An unsettling place, footfall.
People looking a certain way.
Shipfall: still floating?
In darkness the dock buzzes possibility.

Why stay?

The Encounter

It's not so much that you can't learn things in school
As that learning
Turns out to be more like fishing than you might expect.
It needs encounter: not one thing but two.

One sits on the surface, expectant,
Eyes glinting, trying to pierce the reflection,
Harpoon poised to strike any immensity
That comes into view.

The other rises from depths, invisible,
Massive, buoyant now in the act of surfacing,
An impossibly long, rounded body,
Water glistening off fatty flanks
Dropping barnacles and then suddenly
Disengaging pilot fish who can't stand air—

But that's too soon, there's no whale in the story yet,
Only a persuading poet,
Searching waters he can't see or understand.

Oil

Whale oil sweetens the brows of monarchs.
It burns lamps and solidifies soap.
What we know today about this sweet clear fluid
Transforms it from world-circling fuel to mere appetizer,
Whetting maws and furnaces
For the black depths of the earth.

Politics

Top dog's from Nantucket, and Quaker.
Number two's a Cape Codder, and happy.
Third down the line hails from Martha's Vineyard, and angry.

The God-fearing man choses Q. to hurl his spear.
Stubb from the Cape selects Tashtego,
Who hails from the western spur of Flask's own island,
But Flask gives his spear to the African Daggoo.

Three white men in alliance with—
In dominion over—
Three warriors from Indigenous Oceans,
Daggoo's Bight of Benin facing Tash's maritime Massachusetts,
Q.'s vast Pacific glorying around both.

The *P.* sails with worlds sleeping in her belly.
These things must drown.

Knights and Squires

What does I. see when he peers at Knights and Squires?
Can he look past Q.'s beauty, Daggoo's princely bearing,
    Tashtego's Antarctic eyes?
None of the Knights speaks to I., lowly bow-oarsman
And greenhorn that he is.

Does Starbuck signal morality, Stubb boldness, Flask
    endurance?
Do these virtues of mind and spirit
Rule allegorically and painfully over the harpooners?

I. sees them all but issues no commands,
Judges but does not interpret,
Loves but will not move.

[. . .]

He's the center but he's not here.

Left behind—that urgency, focus,
Unrelenting will, drive,
The surge of words, tapping on the wooden deck,
Mad eagerness for revenge and thick heart's blood.

It's hard to sail without.
The deck-ring sits empty in the appointed place.
I. nearly stumbles over it when his watch musters at sunrise.
No ivory peg plumbs that hole,
No hammer smashes no doubloon,
No oaths are taken,
No sacrifices made,
No devils worshipped.

Instead we sail out to sea—to what? Where?
What drives headless *P.* into immensities?
Starbuck's aristocratic bearing, Stubb's cheer, Flask's
    unconsciousness?
Or is it I. alone, high on the masthead,
Shielding his eyes from sun-glitter,
Who steers while sleeping?

Or is there no steering at all?

A Scene on the Quarterdeck

Stubb comes forward as in a play,
Because cheer's the greatest challenge,
Cheer and a vision of common things,
A crew that faces opacity together.

Old age is always wakeful, doesn't say the mad old man
Who's not here.

Stubb wants to pause the tapping
That unrelenting marks time,
Shapes a voyage into a quest for revenge,
Sharpens the harpoon of resentment.

No such rhythms as we sail into unknowing.
Already aloft, I. sees Stubb confused, aimless,
Wandering the quarterdeck as if a grassy plain,
Tall fronds wavering under a steady breeze,
Timid rabbits safe and well-hidden beneath.

No Pipe

Our ship bears no captain.
No captain means no pipe,
No brief instant of repose to be rejected,
No soliloquies to under-passing waves,
No burning embers tossed away,
No hiss in the waves,
No over-passing *P.*
No bubbles descending,
And no return to a not-pegleg's orderly rhythm.

Queen Mab

We sail seeking secrets. Dreams
Come to Stubb in the nightfishing. Not the White Whale
But fantasy's Queen, her tail curling behind,
Beckons to the mate. *Come dance with me,*
She whispers. But the whale-killer cannot
Hear, or maybe he hears but can't remember,
Because even with no captain and no quest
Stubb seeks violence, blood, oil, and other
Liquids for the disassembled casks below,
The empty vessels the journey seeks to fill.

The *P.*, like its mates, ships from New Bedford
And Nantucket, carries coopers to assemble
Casks, frame them with iron hoops into
Open spaces into which the rendered fat
Now turned oil can pour, still hot.

Stubb wakes smelling the Queen's fairy breath.
But a few words with little King-Post
Turn his eyes back to the sea.

No Book

I. needs to make sense of these things:
    Books
    Bones
    Whales
    Glass
    Words
    Pictures
Of what chaos are they constituents?

Once when I. was swimming early in the morning,
Before fishermen or sailors came to share my bay,
I. looked out when I. turned my head and saw
A bird's eye looking back at me.
The devil's cormorant.
Not a creature I. could understand or classify.

The bird sat squat on Whale Rock as I. churned past,
Stroke after stroke. I. kept expecting a flurry of wings
And departure. But the dark eyes followed me,
Or maybe I. anthromorphized that part, but no—
I. believes the cormorant saw me, in my strange wetness
Out of place in the sea.

Walking home the eyes wouldn't leave my mind.

They're gone now.
Just another of the things whose radiant opacity sparked
Into a vanishing fire that marked the leaves of
No book.

Lines of Succession

Why does not Q. captain the *P.*?

No one on board can match him—
His indecipherable tattoos, bronzed glories,
His skill with harpoon in boat or at table,
His love and fearlessness and knowledge
Of so many watery parts of the world.

The tradition about harpooner-officers is Dutch,
In which the fat-cutter or *specksynder*, the chief harpooneer—
On the *P.* that means Q.—
Assumes Starbuck's role as under-captain.

Q. disdains rule. What means command to a body
So free? He pads the deck barefoot and silent,
Weapon always to hand, smelling salt air,
Contemplating blood.

Dinner

Where does Q. eat?

In one scenario he's with the warriors,
The ones that get called barbarians
Not because their speech sounds bar-bar
To sophisticated Greeks, but because the bites
Their sharp teeth take from the life that
Surges around them seem too big
For civilized company.

Or maybe Q. eats alone,
Hidden with his idol someplace deep
In the fo'c'sle, past where I. slings my hammock,
In some recess inside the ship's bulk, known only to
Q., he retires with a bag of spices
That smell of Pacific and the sweat of wild boar,
Dried flesh on which he has been known to feed secretly.

And on happy occasions he may break
His fast with his I.-wife, the two of us on deck
With a warm tropical breeze tickling behind,
Filling the sails with pregnant swell
And forward motion, the lovers meet,
Pass between pale and bronze hands delicate
Handfuls of the flesh of freshly caught fish,
Which crumble to pieces even before passing
Hungry lips.

The Mast-Head

It's my favorite place: vertical, aloft, philosophical.
I. sits and gazes for hours.
So much passes beneath the giant's feet:
The *P.*, the crew, Q., all Knights and Squires,
The press of wind,
The teeming green-glow of upper ocean,
Boiling white in the whaleship's wake.

Beneath foamy stepping stones,
I. imagines a fall into light-bending depth,
Into darkness, weight, profundity.

But that's just the descent.
All around in horizontal directions stretch the glory-curve
And the wonder, its gray surface pocked with
White flecks, surrounding the still-feeling *P.*,
Transforming tiny thinking I. into a spectator
Onto infinity, onto movements and vectors
About which Plato never dreamed,
Onto long lines of birds sketching geometries
Of distance, onto sunglint and side-facing glare,
Onto change and onto changelessness.

I. spies no whales. Not one,
Over the long voyage.

A Spring Rose

No doubloon not-pounded into no mast.
No *intense bigotry of purpose.*
 Bigotry—yes, there is bigotry. The human kind,
 Plural, dissociated, heading in many directions at once.
Somewhat like the glorious *P.* herself.

To sail with no golden goal, no fixed desire,
With only the bloodlust that blood lusts,
Eager but aimless, attracted to flesh and flashing light,
To bodies that are only bodies,
Or if symbols they symbolize the movements
They also perform—

This morning the first yellow rose of spring bloomed in I.'s
 garden.
It won't last.

Sunset

In place of the iron way many turnings.
The sun runs westward, past to future,
The last blaze of color glinting off the dome of Q.'s skull.
How to speak many voices?
Caught as I. remains, imprisoned as myself,
Wishing even now, from the crowded deck,
That I. was alone and aloft,
Seeing from above the way humans look
When they gather together: a pair here,
Trio there, a cluster awkwardly moving past and through
Each other, so many separate worlds
Unable to reconcile.

How do stories end?

Dusk

Starbuck has a bare place in these poems.
His feeble morals vanish with no captain against whom
To contend. His lament for the *heathen crew*
Narrows until he sees
Only Q.'s illuminated back,
Muscles rippling and moving under skin
As he hoists the harpoon in sight of the whale.
Starbuck sees the iron fly,
And he thinks,
"How have I chosen my boat's sharp point?
Will Q. turn the vessel back at me?
Or has my last act been the
Act of choosing, of putting the iron
Into his hand, recognizing his power,
Resigning myself to pagan
Arrowing futures?"

Sometimes I. sees Starbuck looking at the harpooner,
And the bow-oarsman recalls something
He could teach the mate—something about
Love and the human need to
Surrender to that which overmasters.

But mates take no advice from greenhorns
Whether they need advice or no.

First Night Watch

We'll drink tonight, with our feet full light,
    And dance atop the rigging til morn—
Beneath us swim worlds of water!

We'll dance up aloft, with beards tempest-tossed,
    And sway with toes curled in the yards,
High above the waves and swells!

We'll dive, if die we must, and land still alive
    Inside green ocean's arms full rolling,
Down into that saltiest of salty embraces
    That lasts right on til morning!

Forecastle—Midnight

First come two Nantucket Sailors. The rest follow by nations
     and places:
Dutch Sailor, French Sailor, Iceland Sailor, Maltese Sailor,
     Sicilian Sailor,
Long-Island Sailor, Azores Sailor, China Sailor, Lascar Sailor,
Sicilian Sailor, Tahitian Sailor, Portuguese Sailor, Danish Sailor,
English Sailor, Old Manx Sailor, St. Jago's Sailor, Spanish
     Sailor, Belfast Sailor.
Sprinkled among them a few names:
Pip, Tashtego, Daggoo. The voices intermingle
With echoing songs and contrasting colors. The Old Manxman
Fears blackness, but Daggoo takes no offense.

Pip, whose vision's not yet come, sees best:
Midnight brings forth *your white squalls,*
Sudden, violent, constricting, *it makes me jingle*
All over like my tambourine. But now, sailing
Free, without *that anaconda of an old man,*
Into what vistas can those small eyes
Perceive?

Moby-Dick

No swearing and no driving,
No doubloon and no fearless obsession,
No tap-tapping on no quarterdeck,
No quenchless feud spreading its venom
Even into the tepid blood of I. myself—
And yet

The whale swims.

The deep-diver surfaces far from madness.
The incorporate whole, the form and body
Of immensities hidden from human sight.
To such immortality we impute malignancy
As a blanket, covering the hints and properties
That I., asleep at my masthead, fails to spy out.

Faced with the incommensurate, we pose
Choices: obsession and oblivion.
The hunt, the chase, the spear—
Or the languor, the arc, the slow turnings,
The deep dives.

We know which makes the better story.

Great White Evil God

With appalling echoes and Persian fires
He breaches like gunpowder flashing and blinding—
Not so much a color as the visible absence of color—
Until like atheism or milk left too long on a sunny countertop
A thing that until now you could never categorize becomes
All you can see.

Great White Evil God names the prime agent
Indefinite as pain
That markless marks our world.

Now hidden in depths, invisible, White, vanishing—
He's not in the waters but is the Sea—
Great White Evil God is swimming toward your body
Hungering for what lies at the surface.

Would that we could smite Him!
It would be worth soiling the hand that clutches the harpoon
To cast at that infinity
And wound Great White Evil God's body.

It's not to be. He's omnipresent as air,
Heat-trapping as carbon, material as dust, soil, water, spirit.
No sharp tools can prick that flesh.

What does He say to us?
Great White Evil God speaks catastrophes not clauses,
He sings into storms, warbles out waves
That surge away all dryness.
In dreams I. hears Him and deciphers melodies,
And always I. wakes wet
With shivering skin.

Devils Who Never Sleep

Did you hear it?
Don't pretend you didn't hear.
There again. There, there!
Below decks?
Someone coughing in their sleep.
Who sleeps in the middle of the day?
Devils.
Who?
Devils sleep under these decks.
I. sez devils never sleep?
On the *P.* everyone sleeps.
Some sleep during the day.

The Chart

It's an impossible project—
Making a two-dimensional image of
The three-dimensional globe. And it's not just
Curvature that distorts.
The ocean seethes with depth,
Surges with currents and tides,
And in every way frustrates
The chart maker's fixity.

Nonetheless, tools exist.
You lay them flat on a table in the stern cabin,
Plot distances and direction between points
That are never as stable or singular
As they appear on the page.

The chart can focus a monomaniac's attention.
It can seek out white whales
And other monstrosities.
But we are sailing without,
Open to unplans and coincidences
Of comingling and flow.
The complex flatness and mathematical precision
Of rhumbs and meridians and constant angles
Serve not to narrow the chase,
But to display the world's salty plurality—
Mad dynamism, unrepresentable in full,
Emulated in parts.

The Kind of Harpoon I. Throws

The beast at which we strike bleeds history
   Not allegory.
I. casts barbs at living flesh
   Not ideas.

Not Seasick

Lacking its center, our voyage wanders.
His sin was usurpation,
Violent wrenching of authority from its task
Toward a singular purpose,
Our tendency drifts into purposelessness,
Toward vacancy and indolence,
Because what difference makes or time or place,
When all gentle flows make one surging main,
Atop which the *P.* bobs without consequence?

Q. and the Squires dream of blood,
Starbuck and his Knights of money.
Little Pip wishes for comfort,
And the Old Manx Sailor for truth.
But I., sleeping aloft,
Imagines nothing.
Not even sickness.

Weavers

Q. and I. weave together,
Our mat resembles the Loom of Time.
I.'s strong imagination sees myself
As moving shuttle, passing between the
Fixed threads of the warp
In the strong grip of Q.'s brown fingers.
The straight warp of necessity, I. murmurs,
Not to be swerved from its ultimate course,
No matter the plying movements of chance.

Mid-weave the shout comes from Tashtego aloft,
Indian eyes piercing sunglitter:
There she blows!

The First Lowering

Down into boats for violence.
We love it more than we should,
The swirling water and velocity,
The straining after hidden objects,
The staring into eddies below which great creatures
Dive.

We wait, counting the whale's breath,
Eager to strike.

The first lowering amounts to failure.
A sudden squall swamps our boat
And I. and Q. float in a blanket of mist,
Until out of the all-covering cloud
Comes the sharp prow of the *P.*,
Knifing the waters and shattering the boat.

We jump for it, and swim, and live.
Another day.

Testament

I. was the last man brought aboard from the broken boat.
His next project was to draft his will.

Q. was *lawyer, executor, and legatee.*
I. has some objects to dispense.
Item, one book of whales. For Mr. Starbuck.
Item, one pipe. For Mr. Stubb.
Item, one half-whittled nub of wood. For Mr. Flask.
Item, one pen knife. For Pip.
Item, one quire of paper. For the Old Manx Sailor.
Item, one faded newspaper. For Daggoo.
Item, one American nickel. For Tashtego.
Item, one dried-out heart. For Q.

Fedallah

Did we ship the Parsee? Yes.
Leaving the captain behind did not
Abandon his spectral crew.

Fedallah's story is not known.
How did he find the *P.*?
What voyages, what adventures, what epics
Of rise and fall, there and back, out far and
Never to return
Can the *subordinate phantom* speak?

His peculiar ties to the ship,
His disdain for his fellow harpooneers,
His silence,
And his last deep dive

Remain to be interpreted.

The Spirit-Spout

Why choose one Cape over the other?
The *P.* sails toward world-embracing waters.
From New England's bare rocks that means taking
One of two turns.
Either the roaring low hook around Cape Horn,
Or the loping east-bound bend toward Africa, Good Hope
Or Tormentoso, the Cape of Storms,
Where the giant Adamastor
Flexes frustration in surf and froth.

The ship follows a ghostly spout, jetting up
From a spirit-whale, luring them
On by the easier temperate route,
Round Africa to the south and east,
Out of the familiar Atlantic,
Into other spaces.

The *P.* Does Not Meet the *Albatross*

The great Goney-bird is the first ship
Not to see the White Whale.

Aloft I. thinks of the old sailor's song and his bird-
Necklace, of iced-over seas and Life-in-Death,
Of a thousand thousand slimy things,
Of prayer, a Wedding-Guest,
And a compulsion to tell.

I. thinks of this story,
Shifts in his waking sleep-watch,
And forgets to hail the deck.

The *Albatross* sails her unruffled way
North toward Nantucket.

How to Speak Whale

Whales talk over vast spaces—
    Or so cetaceanologists say.
Clicks are for navigation—
    To guide them under the waves.
Whistles are more social—
    To identify pod-mates.
Pulsed calls or squawks broadcast
    The location of giant bodies—
Through light-bending and vision-
    Obscuring depths.

I. sits silent aloft,
Hearing no whalesong.

The Town Ho's Story

Steelkit is the man.
A Lakeman and *desperado from Buffalo.*

Though an inlander, *wild-ocean born.*
Merry as a cricket, he faces Radney's thunder.

He would not do it, he says when Radney
Requires him to sweep the deck. *The deck was not his business.*

Sink the ship? Steelkit cries, while the Captain roars
Turn to! Down in the forecastle, then, down with ye.

Into the maelstrom of injustices
Arises Moby-Dick.

Where Steelkit now is, gentlemen, none know.
But Radney dove deep between the whale's jaws
And his sounding we have not yet heard.

What is a story but an intricate way
Of hiding
Truth?

Monstrous Pictures of Whales

Being monstrous means showing.
Revealing something. Monsters are
Our children—sez the professor—
They greet us at doors to possibility.

Viruses are monsters too.
Birthing winter loneliness.

So—whales, and pictures. I. spends his day-long
Hours aloft and sleeping, not-looking for the
Monstrous cetaceans that he won't-see.
What does a picture of a submerged whale
Look like?

Wandering Southern Ocean waters the way
Thomas Browne wandered fenlands,
Seeking pseudo-knowledge, common
Errors, unseen spouts on unbroken horizons.

Poems can infect imaginations.
And monstrous pictures,
At least some of the time,
Can birth monsters.

Cetacean Errors

To be *less erroneous* means to take fewer
Turns, to sail straight on.
The whales are there,
Whether I. sees them or not.

Interpreting pictures or poems
Echoes but only faintly
The roaring crescendo that arises
When the full body of the sperm whale
Sounds high into air.

Hearing is another seeing,
The splash and rumble that follows the great body
Back into water's embrace.

Whale Rock

They swim everywhere.

Just yesterday I. swam in my bay,
Out past a rocky headland where a neighbor's
New grandson led him a merry chase,
Along a house-filled coast until my path
Crossed Whale Rock.

At high tide the body hides,
And only the outermost hump shows above,
A refuge for gulls and cormorants.
But at the ebb the monstrous frame
Emerges and snakes its way from beach
To water, perhaps eighty feet long,
The span of a great sperm whale dozing
Nose to tail.

I. splashes past awkwardly.
Birds notice.
The whale does not move.

Blue Dreams

What happens when blue floods the green?
When pastoral lyrics become oceanic hymns?
Wishing to be neither elf nor dryad but mermaid and selkie,
Diving deep beyond sight and light,
Into universal cannibalism and terror
Yet still dreaming of ascent
Into light and joy?

Squid

There's a moment in Rich King's great book about *Moby-Dick*,
The title of which I can't reproduce here,
But it rhymes with Mayab's Rolling Sea,
When King himself, master-mariner and teacher,
Grips the pickled arm of a giant squid.
It's all muscle, says his friend the scientist. You ever eat calamari?
King weighs the arm, considers its constricting power,
Touches the suckers
And feels their raspy bite split the latex gloves
The Natural History Museum had pressed
Onto his hands.

Touching the squid—the phantom—
The white ghost—
The harbinger.

The Line

When you become enwrapped in that line,
The rough braids abrading the skin of your shoulder
As rope burns through crotch-bracket,
Its undersea end attached to whale's flesh,
It means knowing by feeling
That the world has its hook
In you.

Stubb Kills a Whale

Our first murder, heart's blood,
Red and spurting out from the killing-lance
Driven home by Master Stubb.
Drowsing I. stands watch on the foremast,
Sleeping again, his soul venturing forth over
Wave-caps and billows. Two other sailors
Napped also—but the whale's spout
Spraying forth in the mid-day air
Like *a portly burgher smoking his pipe*
Of a warm afternoon, awakened all.

Stubb's pipe's smoked too,
By the end. *Both pipes*, said the mate,
Scattering ashes across water.

Authorities

Sailing headless into chaos—
That's what's happening.

When the harpooner strikes the whale,
And the monster dives,
He and the mate switch places.

Gay Header Tashtego's nimble bulk
Dances stern-ward,
While jolly Stubb, lance in hand,
Climbs to the bow.

Who heads the boat?
The warrior or the mate?

It is the harpooner
That makes the voyage,
Intones I.

But the harpooner must labor with pulling oar
Not steering oar.

Stubb only, clenching his pipe,
Stands alongside the dying whale.

Wooden Bodies

It's not just men that kill whales.
Crooked branches, harpoons between their forks,
Hold murder alongside pulling oarsmen.

The v-bends of these crotches grow from American oaks,
Splitting and curving just a certain way,
Selected for that purpose by the keen eye of a landlocked
Ex-sailor, whose own knees no longer serve at sea,
But whose knowledge helps him spy out
Oak knees and crotches suitable for whaling.

We do not sail just as men,
Nor just over oceans.
American timbers bear us,
Craftsmen's irons spring out from our hands,
Manila hemp sits coiled at still harpoon's side.

We are vast, multitudinous, not-only-human.

Eating Whale

Some summers ago in Iceland I. passed a hotel buffet
And thought of long-sunk Stubb.
Most nights
We stayed in hostels or an Airbnb
In Reykjavik. But this morning
We were in a glass-gleaming corporate hotel,
With a dazzling spread.

There between blintzes, cheese, and an unidentifiable
Salami sat rich red rounds of whale.
It looked like nothing so much as *tekka sushi*,
The gleaming flesh of bluefin tuna.

Iceland remains the last spot in Europe
Where whale-flesh nestles near ham and bacon,
Alongside cheeses and fruits, ripe cetacean flesh
Ready to be consumed.

I. ate from the buffet,
Thinking of the mate who bullied the cook,
And of the thoughts, emotions, consciousness
Of the whale that had been.

Cannibal Old Me

Who is not a cannibal?
Spouts know-it-all I., whale-bro, Yankee,
Child of innumerable pinstriped forefathers,
Master of words and arguments,
Eater of flesh.

That I. is, unfortunately, me—
Freed
By the vacancy
That was
[. . .].

Two Shark Stories

Always with a toothsome smile, always mouth-
Open, moving, watching, eyes that
Never close: the shark swims
Under the surface.

What will it take to bring him up?

Sometimes in the Florida heat I. and my son
Fish for sharks with my father.
Captain Bob trails the boat behind shrimp trawlers,
Picking up stray feeders attracted by the blood
And churn.

Once, many summers ago, I. found a four-inch baby
Shark in my home bay in Connecticut,
Plucked it up from the shallows,
Felt its sandpaper skin move in my hand,
And threw it out into deeper water.

Does it swim there still?

Whales and Other Humans

Subcutaneous fat is the thing:
It's what warms whales in icy depths,
And what makes humans human.

Here's the theory:
We're born fatter than other primates,
Squishy soft and luscious. That
Baby-adiposity, the butter under a newborn's skin,
Co-evolved with the voracious energy sink
Of our heavy brains. The mind sucks down the fat
As the child encounters the world's hostilities,
Until the rail-thin teenager must seek fat
Outside the body.

As I. for many years found fat enveloping
The corpses of whales, which the crew would peel back
From dead flesh,
As an orange rind is sometimes stripped by spiraling it.

In the Whalelight

What liquidity, what greasy joy
To wrap oneself in glowing whalefat,
To blaze away Arctic nights and horizon-thin
Daybreaks, to clutch the ooze and crackle
Into oneself, to live safe and insulated
In the whale's fleshbed,
Its caloric covering,
Its oily embrace.

There was a time, in New Bedford,
When streetlights shone clear with sperm oil,
When baleen from bowheads snugged tight each lady's waist,
When clear lubricant greased cotton gins away to the South,
And all of America encased itself in the leavings
Of Leviathan.

That time did not last.

Whalefall

What monuments, what rites, what farewells?
Its buoyancy pierced, the skeleton sinks,
Taking its place in eternal sea-snow,
The accumulation of sediments that assembles
History and ecology and the undersea.
What is I. to make of its unceremonied descent?

Oh, horrible vulturism of earth
I. laments, *from which not the mightiest*
Whale is free!

Whalefalls populate the deep as biomass,
They spiral slowly down to crevasses and scavenger
Bottoms. Fish and crabs and bivalves follow, alongside deep-sea
    creatures
Whose outlines we can barely envision.

The whale fashions its own monument.

The Whale's Head

He's not there to say to it:
O head!
Thou hast seen enough to split the planets
And make an infidel of Abraham,
And not one syllable is thine!

When the foremost chunk of whaleflesh jangles from the
    side-chains
The *P.* might be said
To have a head
But no captain.

No turns on the quarter-deck.
No pausing, no striking with Stubb's long spade,
No eyes not fixed attentively on the head
That is also a symbol
Even when its flesh stinks
And attracts birds.

No voicing of no analogies, dim recollections
Of the self that was left onshore,
Or the body slowly wafting down
To unseen depths.

No Tail on the *Jeroboam*

The ship's from Nantucket
Bearing the angel Gabriel.

You remember the story
Of the shipmate ensorcelled by the Shaker God
And devoted to the nameless whiteness
Swimming in the whale.

Gabriel prophesized death, for the *Jeroboam*'s mate
And the captain we sail without.

What says he now, to a *P.* without a head?
With many blasphemers but no God-rebel,
No urgent violence on the quarterdeck,
No doubloon embedded in the mast.

Sail on, ye mariners, shouts the befuddled angel,
But beware of the horrible tail!

The Monkey-rope

Being wedded to Q. is the best thing on the voyage.

It's easy for I. to spot him.
The harpooners berth aft, with the officers,
And I. the green hand nestles in the crowded for'c'sle.

Sometimes they rendezvous early
Or in glowing twilights of calm evenings,
To talk and smoke and avoid prying eyes.

The monkey-rope fashions a working marriage,
In which Q.'s beauty shows to uncommon advantage
While I. above surrenders to the line.

Its elongate Siamese ligature creates
A sort of interregnum in Providence,
So that whatever fate would strike the cannibal

Strikes I. too. The bow oarsman keeps close watch
On his pagan bedmate. When the shark's teeth snaps
I. jerks the rope, pulling Q. back from danger,

For a time.

Brothers in Arms

Flask: What's a whale, friend?
           Why do we kill them?

Stubb: Like rightness, the whale exceeds us.
           We spy him from above, dream
           About his deep dives and the mist
           Of his sounding. To be the right
           Whale means to float, to be fat
           And full of blubber, to sport a smile
           Full of umbrellas and corsets.

Flask: But must they bleed?
           I've seen the red flood in the water,
           And I've heard the calves crying
           To their lost mothers.

Stubb: It's a world of blood, King-Post.
           I didn't make it.

The Sperm Whale's Head

His high forehead batters the world
Which is Ocean.

Eyes separated by tons and expanse,
Ears hidden in tiny holes,
Rows of shiny-sharp teeth.

Harpooners draw these teeth with practiced knives.
Forty-two in all, and undecayed.

Q. slashes the gums with a cutting-spade,
And the whale's flesh-eaters lie open.

Drawn teeth retell the story
With violence refashioned as decoration.

I. wishes for that shapely
An ending.

The Right Whale's Head

Baleen hoops this jaw
Shaped like a bass-viol.

Solid like the trunk of a giant oak
The Right Whale's head sports
A crown above,
A pouting lower lip
Baleen-filled,
And inside, following Jonah's road
Into the hidden shelter,
Through the *hogs-bristles* or *blinds* that strain away everything
    but food,
Into the invisible stomach.

I. takes the domed forehead of the Sperm for Platonism, and
The full lower lip of the Right to quiver Stoic resolve.

The *P.* seeks the meat-eater and its lust for meaning,
And disdains placid filter-feeding stoicism.

But when Q. gives up his spear into whaleflesh
And blood boils red in the cold water,
It's hard to read either Platonic lure
Or Stoic resignation
In the splash of water and foam.

I.'s Blue

There's a hidden desire in I.'s yarn
About the time the Sperm Whale's battering ram Head
Stove a passage through the Isthmus of Darien
And mixed the Atlantic with the Pacific.

To I., that Sperm-made mixing represents
The real and only truth of the World
Which he calls Ocean.

There is neither Atlantic nor Pacific,
Neither enclosed Med nor icebound Arctic,
Only one endless flowing body
Sloshing forever atop Earth's rocky carcass.

From aloft I. marvels at expanse and sunlight.
Into this eternity the Sperm Whale's Head
Batters a path that is Time itself,
Heading only its own way
Into oblivion.

Let the Oil Out!

Let flesh be light!
Spermaceti blazes best,
The clearest, brightest, the most insightful,
Neither smell nor smoke
But only glistening, pure.

Even the shadows its light casts
Outline themselves with precision.

As if by that light and that light only
I. sees into the heart of things,
Ocean's wet soul
And constant motions.

Birthing Tash

Tashtego falls. I. allegorizes:

Inside the Head a trapped Indian struggles.
The whalemen spy him throb and heave
Inside the massive case as it hangs alongside the *P.*

It is as if, thinks philosopher I.,
The Head were at *that moment seized*
With some momentous idea.

The tackle parts.
Head splashes into the sea.
Q. dives to the rescue,
Delivers Tash from whaleshead womb.

The Gay Header does not speak of entombment
But I. dreams of having *likewise fallen into*
Plato's honey head, and sweetly
Perished there.

I. still dreams of it.
As if the Whale himself might surface
And speak.

Read It If You Can

Is the Whale a Genius?
Pysiognomically regarded, I. must demur.
He has no proper nose, and lacks
Q.'s true George Washington grandeur.

But the prairie of brow,
Milk-soft and undulating,
Resists interpretation.

What can we read in a face,
In *the awful Chaldee of the Sperm Whale's brow?*

I. does not know.
I. can't stop reading.

A Hill of Snow

Above the first vertebra
Rises that slight hump,
The distinctive convexity
Of the White Whale,
Amid always-moving sea.

What kind of a book is the whale?
What decipherings follow in his foamy wake,
Stretching in ever-opening V's to sternward,
Until they sink into water's own movement,
Alien, without intention, physical,
Endless, enticing?

What maps map his swimming?
Atop what snowy hilltops can we see
A skein of passages organize themselves
Into design?

The P. Meets the V.

On the sea the *P.* sometimes meets other boats.
One such, the *V.*, lights no oil and pricks no flesh.
They gam, and spy, and lower.
The *V.* will not give way to the *P.*
But the skilled harpooners of the *P.*
Looping span the *V.*'s boats and strike fast.
The whale killed, the *P.* finds a stone harpoon
In his flesh: *It might have been darted by some*
Nor'West Indian long before America was discovered.

No more discoveries of whale-past. The *P.*
Now lists with an immovable sinking corpse alongside.
Q.—at times like these it is always Q.—cracks the chain
And releases the *P.* with the carpenter's hatchet.

And the *V.*, forlorn, sails off in pursuit
Of a spout that's not vendible Sperm
But escapable Fin-back.

The Honor and Glory of Whaling

Just now I. puts my pale naked speculating body
Into salt water. On the first full flood
Of summer, I. swims cross-ways to the incoming
Tide, out past a rocky headland,
Along Whale Rock,
Which today only peeks low granite humps
Above the waves.

I. will swim farther out today—
All the way to the center of the map
Where the Cow & Calf,
Two rocks of different sizes,
Nestle contemplatively
Between worlds.

To swim means not to drown, repeatedly.
To put one's bare body into cold water.
To subject one's movements
To the circulating ebbs of the moon
And the dream of buoyancy.

Just now, for a secret long hour,
Face down, shoulders rotating,
Vision compressed into gray-green haze
Faintly back-lit by a sun just past noon,
I. words myself into the wonder.

No spears on these rocks,
Not today
Or any day.

Jonah Historically Regarded

Think of that instant, that beach-moment,
When the prophet, stinking of bile and righteousness,
Vomit-hurled onto shore,
After three days inside and beneath,
Speaks.

What does he know, Jonah, of time and place?

Depth means insight,
A richer, thicker, heavier knowledge,
Unavailable to the thin climes of air
And alphabets,
Decipherable only in the body,
Tattooed with darkness,
Of the man who dove deepest.

Listen to him,
I. begs you.

Just a Little Farther

Sometimes you want to extend your reach.
The whale lies beyond your grasp,
That great mass of flesh, blubber, and money—
So you pitchpole your lance.

It means balancing the weapon's dull end
Upon upraised palm,
Extending the killing point high into the air,
Until in a juggler's rush
The lance jerks and soars,
High arcing across the intervening waves,
And the gray back spouts red blood.

Stubb chortles, gamesome, talks,
While the whale dies.

How We Breathe

It's what even I., dozing, sees when it's pointed out to I.—
A foamy white burst at the water's surface,
Misting the horizon's broad edge
And waking the sleepiest of Pantheists.

I. sees it when it's close,
As in a mirror held before my face,
Invisible droplets stain the glass,
The water that's in every mouthful of air,
Two elements intermingled,
Light and dry air meets wet and heavy water,
And together our contaminated respiration
Writes visible traces
For everyone to see.

The Tail

Because we cannot gaze upon his forehead
That blank eyeless grayness
We fix detail-starved eyes upon
The tail.

The tail is Motor, Mace, Sweep, Lobtail,
And visible sign Flukes.

It's what we see,
What makes us desire,
What we can't follow.

The Grand Armada

Breasting the straits of Sunda, the *P.* arrives
At a magical meeting
Where whale-mothers and nursing calves desport
Themselves in *dalliance and delight.*

Not a lance was thrown, though Q.
Reached tattooed hand into the water
To stroke a gray forehead.

And I., watching, gazes upon amours
He cannot touch, and wishes
Myself whale.

A Love Story

Among whales, solitude is for old bulls,
Conviviality for mothers and calves.

But on board the *P.*, solitude
Is for him we left behind.

Flashes of the convivial appear at odd moments,
When I. glimpses Q. on an afternoon watch.

Sparks run as he sharpens his harpoon.

His body shines with moisture and light.
Muscles shimmer under brown skin
Like thoughts enfleshed.

And in that flash and instant, that passing,

The entire whaleship, the world, the ocean,
Quiver with love.

Fast-Fish and Loose-Fish

It's a story about fishing, and about the law.

The Fast-Fish *belongs to the party fast to it.*
The Loose-Fish *is fair game for anybody who can soonest catch it.*

From these precepts flow all ownership and regulation.

What is the great globe itself but a Loose-Fish? sez I.,
Warbling imperial ambivalence.

Meanwhile Q. sharpens his barb,
Stares at the blank surface,

And dreams of the hunt.

Heads or Tails

To whom the spoils, the head or the tail?

The King claims Head, with its case of spermaceti.
The Queen chooses Tail, with its sinuous force.

Does that Tail transform Queen into mermaid?
Wonders mischievous I.

Would it transform me?

The P. Meets the Rose Bud

The flower-named ship stinks of death.
Blasted corpse on one side,
And dried-out whaleflesh on the other.

Stubb knows the game.
The French captain sails off whale-less,
While the *P.* generously tows the dry corpse
Under its lee.

The mate spades into the smell,
Digging furiously, shielding the revealed meat
From *numberless fowls*,
    Until his own nose discerns
Amid the stench and decay,
A faint stream of perfume.

Six fat handfuls of ripe Windsor ambergris soap,
One for each Knight and heretical Squire,
And more still might have been sought,
Had not the wind blown the *P.*'s head down,
Backed her into the miasma,
From which good Starbuck ordered new sails raised
And headway made.

Ambergris

There is an unctuousness on the far side of decay,
From which it emerges.

Out of the decaying Head
Grows fragrance.

Does this sweet cheese comprise the true heart of the whale?
Do the flukes of the Sperm Whale dispense such perfume,
So that the death we seek in rushing waters
Finds our noses before
Our hearts?

The Castaway

Pip overboard!

Alone in the sea a boy suffers.

What does he see, floating at water's level?
Not I.'s masthead horizon,
Nor Q.'s target of oil and muscle,
Nor the blacksmith's anvil—when you hold a hammer,
All the world's anvils—

No, Pip sees depth:
The multitudinous (cue the *Macbeth* music)
God-omnipresent (because absence is presence)
coral insects (which he thinks are not living at all)
that out of the firmament of waters heaved the colossal orbs.

We pick up the boy, his body at least.
It chances that the hand that reaches out to him
In the water belongs to I.,
And in Pip's frozen face I. sees a vision
Of an *uncompromised* (because unaware)
Soul, *indifferent as his God.*

We take him back aboard,
Though he frights all of us except Q.,
Who nothing feared,
And who amuses himself by slicing
For the boy choice bits of whale gristle
With his well-honed harpoon.

A Squeeze of the Hand

To be a body is to want not to be
Alone.

There comes a time when whalemen
Work the flesh,
When I. joins with foc's'le hands
When Q. is belowdecks spearing whalesteaks,
A red sun dips below slate-still water,
And the men sit together and squeeze.

Squeeze, til you split yourself!
The dream of solitude, the vision of separate
Selves, each one inside his own
Skin, but squeezing sperm together,
As if to sit and squeeze were to build
A mechanism to let the self out,
To set the self free,
To go outside each our solitary bodies and
Skins—but not far outside,
No farther than the hands
Of the man sitting next to you,
Clumsy, calloused hands, but now
Sweetened and slippery with sperm,
As if they are I.'s hands and also not-I.'s,
Extensions of his-self and your-self,
Prosthetic grips into a world whose violence
Hides itself for a short and fragrant time
Beneath squeezing and trembling hands.

The Cassock

Jet-black as Q.'s Yojo,
The grandissimus embraces a mincing sailor
And protects his body as
Robes do an Archbishop.

Under the sheltering cover of the whale's penis-
Skin, we might wonder—
What is the sailor?

Is he the hidden body,
His skin brown or bronze or pale or black or yellow?

Is he a speculating mind,
Soaring thoughts out and past the masthead?

Is he a hidden face,
Eyes gleaming through slits in the mighty foreskin?

Or is there no sailor at all,
But only an act of investiture,
Only the shell of the whale's massive organ,
Only a membrane regulating the oily world's sparks and fires,
Only the costume, never the actor.

I. fears the skin-robe
And refuses my turn to wear it.

The State of the Ship

Pots of bubbling oil simmer amidships,
Tiny bits of whale's body,
Minced, sliced, fried, and at last
Rendered liquid and viscous—oil
For the benediction of Nantucket lamps.

When I. observes the *P.* in full tumult,
Smoking fires, bubbling try-pots,
Harpooners gesticulating,
The ship champing the white bone of
Her bow-wave beneath as she
Burns whale's flesh in her belly—
Everywhere afire with a miasma that transforms
Life into fuel,
He sees unity.

But the *P.* sails under no command,
Seeks no symbols,
Burns only I.'s own fires.

The Lamp

What if the light I. seeks isn't oil but interiority,
An inward-seeking clarity, a mirror—
But one that does not reflect universal light
But instead generates its own luminosity
And shines within?

So much depends upon light from without!
Our puddled earth itself, ellipsing its way
Around the ball of fire from which
We capture the barest conic fraction
Of light and heat, generates no light
From its own lamp.

Unless—here is the secret maybe—
There is a hidden lamp also,
Not rendered from whaleflesh nor
Dredged from dark Satanic pits,
But clear and warm and concealed
Inside each sailor's flesh,
Behind the stomach
Tucked in alongside liver or gall bladder,
There's a human shared
Light—
That traces itself over night-seas
To show the way?

If such stomach-oil exists and can be burned,
Or can light its own fires and cast thin shadows,
Then surely the harpooners are the
Most-barreled bulls—
Daggoo's gleaming torso hides gallons of light,
Tashtego's long hair cascades down bronze shoulders
Afire with light, and most of all Q.—

Beloved Q.—
Conceals in cannibal body
A skein of lights, a winking network
And guide to the salt-water labyrinth,
If only we can read the way.

The Search

Something's missing on the *P.*

The sailors look everywhere:
In each cask of still-warm oil stowed belowdecks,
Inside the iron vacancies of the try-pots,
Beneath the embers of the coal fires,
In half-assembled hoops of casks
And in the froth of blood, oil, and seawater
That stains the decks.

Like a decapitated corpse or the still water
At the just-now pause of flood-tide,
The *P.* moving feels herself still, settled,
Without urgency.

Beneath her keel Ocean flows silently
And without thoughts.

No Doubloon

No gold coin mars or marks our mast.
No old man is *firm tower* or *volcano*.
No mutterings from the mates or the crew
Follow behind soliloquizings
Or punctuate his mad focus.

What's a doubloon worth on an open sea?

Maybe it's the double in the coin
That entrances. As if the gold thing
Can be two places at once,
Or occupies two times—because gold means the future,
Things that can be purchased and held
In future times and climes,
Safe
Against future catastrophes and horrors.

To sail with no money in the mast
Means trusting ourselves to futures
Without hidden stores,
Encountering horizons
With no stockpiles,
And ranging into unknown waters
Without the consoling presence
Of a home-facing dream.

The P. *Meets the* Samuel Enderby *of London*

The *P.* meets the dis-armed *Samuel Enderby.*
Spin the yarn, we say.
Where didst thou see the White Whale?
Because even captainless we yearn for news
Of Moby-Dick, glimpses of flash and force—
Great White Evil God.
We don't call him that because no names pass our lips,
Fedallah sits mute,
As our voyage arcs toward the greatest of open seas.

Seeing how matters stood, says the English captain,
I resolved to capture him,
The noblest and biggest whale I ever saw.

The Londoner catches a glimpse,
Starts his great dive,
But the harpoon's *barb ript its way along the flesh*
And up the stranger floats, spared, armless, living.

He has a theory of godhead: *What you take for the White Whale's*
      malice
Is only his awkwardness.

We don't say what [. . .] would say—
He's a magnet—
But high aloft, staring down at Q.,
As the Squire straddles the rail with one foot dangling
      ocean-ward,
Sharpening his harpoon with musical scrape,
I. feels the attraction.

The Next Voyage

There will come a time,
An after-time, as this is before-time,
When the bottle will stand full,
The table crowded,
The breeze fresh and horizon clear—
A time when the voyage
Will not pass under death's shadow
Nor through the prickly corona of virus,
But instead will glide into open seas,
Unbroken by whale spouts,
Capped by rows of waves,
Into which I. points his ship-self
In the hope of discovering
Things the *P.* never found.

Inside the Skeleton

To walk under any arch means entering into
Some unknown, some mystery,
As when I., long since off the *P.* and wandering,
Rambles tattooed limbs onto the island
Of Tranque (don't check your map)
And inside the framing skeleton
Of the Sperm Whale.

Not that Whale, of course, who for all we know
Swims still, inviolate as Whiteness—
But some other giant stranded on a beach in the Arsacides
Whose bleached bones arc over I.'s head,
Cross-hatching the shade and perforating tropical sun.

What does I. feel inside those ribs,
Upright in Jonah's cave,
Pacing back and forth inside
The colonnades?

To bear a body's witness is not enough.
I. must also measure.

Measurement of the Whale's Skeleton

What does God come to, in so many inches?

If the seventy-two-foot skeleton indicates a ninety-foot
Whale,
What ratio of flesh over the bones abstracts itself into
Divinity?

Viz., ribs, ten on a side, the first six feet long—
    A mannish size—
Viz., a length of naked spine echoing flukes-ward,
Viz., forty and odd vertebrae
    The smallest of which long since disappeared
    As marbles for Tranquean children.

Child's play, sez I.

The Fossil Whale

What is immortality but ubiquity in time?

Deep backward into stone impress
Traces of Whale carve themselves,
Bones transfigured into granite,
Once-arching ribs into squat pillars,
Broken and scattered into black Alabama soil,
The fertile southland above which Leviathan
Once swam,
When all the world was a water-spanned
Sphere,
A blue-green mantle covering lands
That would one day sprout men.

Swim with these words,
Sound to your song,
Stone-still and flowing,
Until its rhythms splash
Wet
Across this page.

Save the Whales!

There are two possibilities.
One is the story I. knows.
The other is the one I. believes.

Whales grow thin as the *P*. weathers the African Cape.
They no longer present spouts to shore-bound Basque
  whalemen,
Nor to Nantucketers in near-shore haunts.
Whaleships pursue the beasts into blue emptiness,
Chasing them at last into polar vastnesses, north and south.

But I. believes not in extinction.
No steel barb, though hurled by Q. himself,
And the killing spade plunged by Starbuck,
Could exterminate the world-circling monster,
Who *in Noah's flood despised Noah's ark*,
And who spouts *frothed defiance* above the equatorial flood.

How to reconcile what I. knows and what I. believes?
  We account the whale immortal in his species,
However perishable in his individuality.

Like all of us,
I. lies to myself.

Glass Foot

Not transparent to see through but fragile. Light-latticed.
About to fracture. It strains its way beneath you, bending
And then turning abruptly, sliding on wet snow—
Woomph—
And down you go.

What is it like to live shore-bound with a glass foot?
Too much of feeling hast thou—
Too jagged the edges of tide press sand down,
Until a blaze of red transfigures sky and sense,
And with too much heaviness you fall.

To be a foot among bottles!
Free and unremarkable, surrounded by excess, by broken things,
By light that bends and scatters and screams.
On sand that's not yet glass and leather that never will be
Circumambulating you labor an island's circumference.
Each step a bitter flame and movement.

On this beach being seen through means just seeing.
Not breaking.

The Carpenter

Because we need to build something.
Not all the things that we left without
Can join us—but building itself,
Carpentry as labor and process,
That's been on the *P.* all along.

His brains ooze into his fingers,
That's what I. sez about the wood-
Worker, part-joiner, the one who makes.

Because I. knows that when
You sail headless into chaos
Into the surge and tumble of the sea
And all it's worth—
When that open-ness attracts
Your compass needle
And that sudden shift beneath the keel
Moves your boat
Then, you need a carpenter.

He's a practical man.

What the Carpenter Says

What does the maker say to vacancy?
The dialogue concerns *old Adam,*
The offending part that makes man man,
And the abiding question about whether
Technology
Can displace it.

Item, one ivory leg: gone.
Item, one spyglass: in Starbuck's hands.
Item, one Nantucket hat: on Stubb's head.
Item, one killing lance: between Flask's fingers.

Might all the captain's parts—
Most of the captain's parts—
Sail separately?

The maker's task,
Subdued to what it works in,
Brings to the *P.*'s glory and variety,
An adhesive force, a voice,
That *one sufficient little word queer,*
As the carpenter murmurs Stubb's phrase,
While filing down the leg we don't need,
To be fitted into a hole on the deck that's not in use,
Fixing eyes trapped on a distant American shore
On that snowy hump that may yet sound
Out of the ocean's gray horizon.

Starbuck in the Cabin

The moral crisis: can he murder
In service of the greater good?

No answer comes from no ruling deity.
The *P.* sails godless.
Casks of oil leak in the hold.

Starbuck drinks coffee.

Q. in His Coffin

Fevers seize even Q.,
Even unconsciousness
Falls into chills and visionary knowledge.

A coffin prepared. Yojo's blessing. Q.'s body.

The crew gathers around an idol.
The lid closes.
Pip cries out, *Poor rover*!
Starbuck requests *heavenly vouchers.*
Let's make a General out of him! shouts the boy,
Shifting Q. from open sea to bloody field.

I. stares at the coffin and speaks no words.

Q. does not die game,
But adopts empty coffin as sea chest
And spends idle hours absorbing I.'s eyes
While carving onto coffin-wood the indecipherable tattoos
That beautify his living skin,
A wondrous work in one volume,
Answers to riddles not even I. can speak.

The Pacific

Utopia floats
Near I., where I. dream-swims every night.

Liquid, alluring, *mysterious, divine,*
It zones the world's whole bulk about
And goes erroneously by the name of peace.

Two places swim toward each other.
The realm of Pan,
I.'s many voices and god-spirit-guide.
And the globe-embracing waters in which
Even now swims
The White Whale.

Things must collide.
Even here.

The Blacksmith

Named Perth,
After a city by the River Tay
Or one upriver from the gentle rollers of the Indian Ocean,
Or still yet a New Jersey port town, industrial and polluted,
A place to which I. once sailed through a storm
With my now-dead uncle who served in the Coast Guard.

Blacksmiths like carpenters are makers,
But iron requires more heat than joining wood.

Perth left in grassy graves onshore a wife and two children.
Before him opened nothing but the whale's road.

Making a Harpoon

To bind iron for a whale
Requires skin-scalding fire,
Smoldering black smoke
Trailing its acrid cloud behind the *P.*'s stern,
Twelve twisted rods,
Heated to make them red with flex,
Combined into a whole that shows no distinctions,
A *tow-line* to fix white whaleflesh
And unbearable weight.

Pagan harpooneers give blood
For *the true death-temper.*

Not in the name of any father—
      The *P.* sails with no fathers—
Nor in the names of sons—
      Whose wayward names must be hidden—
But under devil-sign,
      Fires of suffering
Held in painful unity
      At the final barbed point
Of the killing spear.

Calenture

The sea smells land-like today,
As I. swims past Whale Rock,
Eying the birds.

Three black cormorants face into the wind,
While three white gulls point their beaks away.

After so much immersion in water and words,
So much thinking-with and accommodation
To the fluid form that buoys I. up,
So many orphan souls reclaimed,
Named and known even if laboriously—
But maybe it's the swimming that works after all?
Arms churn and feet kick out
A flutter rhythm.

I. has my own knowledges,
Head-down in green water.
Each day I. swims the same direction.
Out!

The P. Meets the Bachelor

A full ship and homeward-bound, they don't believe
In the White Whale.

What's it like to live in that glitterworld?
To plough oceans without malice,
In search of a Great God who's neither Evil
Nor White.

Starbuck loves to think he loves such a God,
But I. swims past Whale Rock,
Into a slight chop raised by the north wind,
The salt-spume scattering when I. reaches my left arm
Forward
And the froth splashes
Into my open mouth
Just then gasping down
The necessary air.

No direction is homeward-bound,
Not for the *P.*
Nor I.

The Dying Whale

Behind the swimmer,
Or the whale,
Or the *P.*,
The wet track widens.

In the wake of any movement
A "V" of action past
Opens, increases, expands,
Yawns its jaws apart,
Rippling across the surface,
Back and still back.

It's not the direction that I. swims.
Facing the water, I. cannot see
The expanding track I. makes on
Ocean's ruffled face.

That back-facing open wake
Marks the *P.*'s journey
For every wet mile,
Every barrel of light and heat,
Every spear darted and oar pulled.

What happens if swimmer or ship stops,
Raises head above the swell,
And surveys back-facing the opening his progress
Has marked?

When It's Almost Possible To See

On full moon summer nights
      Like tonight
It becomes almost possible to see
      Through moon glow
The path the *P.* takes across
      Wave roads
Toward polyglot futures.

Listen!
      (The waves lap.)
Can you hear?
      (The wind splashes.)
I. wants to go there!
      (Whale Rock does not move.)

Six birds, sitting.
Clustered close on the narrow outcrop that
Must be the whale's tail,
They face separate ways
Into wind and sun.

I. swims past,
Face beneath the surface.

The Quadrant

Smash it!
Who needs machines?
I. knows where the sea is
And where I. floats in it—

The quadrant tells an old tale,
Fixed points in the sky,
Stars to the wandering bark,
Looking on tempests,
Never shaken.

That's not the way I. swims.

To shake and be shaken
Gives the true destination—
        Remember: there's no gold in our mast—
Because buoyancy embraces turbulence,
Motion that holds things up.

To fix starry body from swelling sea
Tells a universal story
That I. the swimmer,
Ears clogged with saltwater,
Arms churning,
Feet splashing in time,
Cannot hear.

Swimmer in the Storm

And into the firestorm sails the *P*.,
Into emptiness of summer afternoon,
Air crackling with anticipation,
Clear spirit of fire rolling in behind
Hammerhead clouds.

Yesterday I. sat on a rock above the beach,
Watching lightning fork its delicate touch
From cloud to grayswell,
Marking a photo-negative of the wonderworld,
So briefly visible,
So insubstantially touched.

I. wanted to dive into storm-raised waters
But I. did not.

The Deck Towards the End
of the First Night Watch

There's no view during the storm.
The sailors grapple the brain-truck
In tempest-time.

Midnight—The Forecastle Bulwarks

I wonder, muses Stubb,
Whether the world is anchored anywhere?

Flask the King-Post has no answer,
All he offers to storm and night
Is feeling
Bare sensation,
Skin that feels the drive of rain,
The pin-prick pressure of wind-driven
Droplets on his face.

A feeling man in the tempest
Contributes nothing.

If she is, continues the middle mate,
She swings with an uncommon long cable.

Midnight, Aloft—Thunder and Lightning

We don't want thunder. We want rum. Give us a glass of rum!

Errors in a Book

The book on the shelf knows what you are thinking.
Squat toad in a dry cistern, it's got more inside than outside,
More leaves than branches,
More heart than shell.

I. wants to know which way to turn!

Other voyages swim into view
As I. watches islands and shores pass away.
I. hears no peg-leg's tapping,
Staccato but faint,
Asking that I. turn and follow,
But giving no direction.

She's a monster, the poet says,
Book-vomiter with a serpent's body,
Brood-eater.

Also a way to keep score in baseball . . .

Can we turn but not into catastrophe?

Errant, erring, erroneous:
Of meanings not parsimonious
Nor harmonious
More like Polonius
Than like Hamlet.

The end is near.
Around the corner
Or on the other side of the page
Just one more turning,
One more mistake,
And you're not there.

At Sea

What is direction out of sight of land?
To be boundless
Disoriented
When tooth-rows of white
Lap the Nantucket wood
Of the angular bow.

Sometimes a storm inverts the needle
Because the directions West
And East
Are arbitrary, map-maker's
Conventions,
Impositions of direction
On the all-exceeding expanse
Of surge and mirrors.

On the masthead not-seeing across wideness
I. ignores the needle—
Done with the compass!
Done with the chart!

The Log and Line

Needles and maps are not the only guides.
Behind the stern opens a mouth,
Frothy V. of vacancy refilled,
Water in-rushing and space conquered.

The Manxman heaves the log,
The reel spins,
Ocean surges beneath the keel.

When the line parts
It's no surprise to I.
The *P.* has long since jumped
Into sea-embracing.

Only Pip cries at the log's vanishing,
For the boy sees in that bobbing
Bit of wood, vanishing astern,
Image and memory
Of his own body,
Wet and alone,
Eyes dry and open,
Fearing the multitudes
That lie beneath.

The Life-Buoy

An anonymous man drowns—
      First of the *P.* to mount the mast
      On Moby-Dick's peculiar ocean
Takes with him the ship's life-buoy.

Q. has an answer to everything.

His coffin, caulked and sealed,
Contains no beautiful body
But buoyancy's airy heart.

The carpenter doesn't like it,
But Q. doesn't mind—
Cannibal teeth flash in the sun
As he watches his body's container
Splash through the waves.

Coffins

To re-fashion coffin into life-buoy
Takes nothing but art.
The carpenter applies caulk to the seams,
Then black pitch, to hold the seal,
And the boat that would have sailed Q.'s body to the stars
Floats.

What does the carpenter think?
At sea, wood carries everyone—
No one lives absent wood-shaped embrace,
Swell of the hull,
Ribs of the whaleboat,
Eruptions of mast,
Awkward joinings of knees and joints.

For the *P.* too is pitch-sealed, tightly-caulked
And a coffin
As I. knows from
The distant smile
That flutters over Q.'s lips
Early on a Pacific morning.

The P. *Meets the* Rachel

Hast seen a whale-boat adrift? says the stranger captain
Who's looking for someone else.

Now in the White Whale's own waters,
Placid, Pacific, opaque,
Ruffled by variable breezes
The *P.* encounters symbols.

The *Rachel* has lost her children
And will not be comforted.

The stranger captain offers money, wine, oil,
Asks only for time,
That the *P.* join his futile search
Through the sea's worth,
Sifting foam and salt to seek
One precious boy,
Who is not.

The *P.*'s bow-wave slices downwind,
Q. and I. stand at the stern,
Looking into a "V"
Opening wider until the stranger boat
Disappears.
I. reaches for Q.'s hand
But the cannibal has caught the scent
And he scrambles forward
Without seeing.

Pip in the Cabin

With no singularity inside it, the cabin
Smells wet and salty.
Pip enters, shivering.
He whispers
To unhearing wooden walls.

Shame on all cowards, squeaks the boy
To an all-judging Father
Who is not there
And does not hear.

No Hat

No captain mounts no mast,
None determines to hoard to himself
The first sight of air-seeking
Whiteness on the white-capped horizon.
No *red-billed savage seahawk*
Snatches no Nantucket hat
From no gray-fringed head.
No bird flies into obscurity,
Clutching no prize.
Bearing no traces of human habiliments
The bird crosses no invisible lines,
Does not shimmer into indistinction,
Drops no *minute black spot*
From no *vast height*
Into no sea.

The P. *Meets the* Delight

Last ship but one,
And she's *Delight*,
But no delight has she had since
Encountering Moby-Dick.

Four stout sailors dived down with
The White Whale, and a fifth, wrapped in sailcloth,
Splashes from the rail
Into anonymous depths.

The forward-braced *P.* leaps out
With the breeze, but cannot escape
The *ghostly baptism*
Sprinkled by the shrouded whaleman-corpse that makes
A final dive.

The last of the stranger captains,
Eyeing the *P.* as she sails on,
Spots Q.'s coffin lashed sideways on the taffrail,
And knows, as we all know,
Which way the whaleship sails.

The Symphony

The *feminine air*
And
The *masculine sea*
Spread themselves
In front
Of the eager *P.*

This is the magic glass, man,
No captain says to Starbuck.

Where do murderers go, man,
Intones no sonorous voice,
Wrestling with Fate.

But it is a mild, mild wind,
That blows the *P.* toward divinity.

Who's to doom,
When the judge himself is dragged to the bar?

No sailor sails alone.
We collaborate with wind and sea and sky,
Under the skein of heaven,
In the company of differences.

The Chase—First Day

Since [. . .] is not here to steal the seeing,
Tashtego raises Moby-Dick.
He wins no doubloon but gains a sight
Of flashing sunglister—
The bodily glare of Great White Evil God
As he so divinely swam.

Why should we not seek his body?
Why not out of thirty, make one man?
Straining at oars,
Splashing across a gentle swell,
Daggoo's broad back visible
Even to I., who labors my bow oar,
Mere inches from Q.'s coiled frame,
Eager to exchange oar for harpoon
And to cast at that infinity.

The whale's jaw snaps boat-ribs.
Men scatter.
Stubb counts five floating oars
And numbers five rescued men.

Away to leeward spume rises
Once, twice, to reveal direction,
Then two incandescent flukes catch the sun's last light,
Flash defiance at the *P.*,
And dive.

The Chase—Second Day

From below
The *P.* echoes faintly,
Just a blip of sonic reply,
A ghost of a ship
Protruding wooden keel into
An ocean of sound.

The White Whale hears—
The muffled green texture
Of floating kelp
And the silver bellies
Of flying fish piercing the surface.

The White Whale hears—
The sideways perambulations
Of scavenging crabs
And the profundity of cogitations
Of the octopus in its cave.

The White Whale hears—
The bottlenose dolphins'
High-pitched squawk
And the frenzied scatter
Of deep-water mackerel.

The White Whale hears—
The rustle of wind
Disturbing ocean's surface
And the ninety-degree turnings
Of the cuttlefish.

The White Whale hears—
The mourning cry of
The pelican mother
Who nurses her young with the blood
Of her own breast.

The White Whale hears—
The naked feet of Q.
As the harpooneer descends
The masthead for the last time,
His eyes scanning
For I.'s face.

The White Whale hears—
Endless permutations of soft-bodied
Jellyfish, as they prepare
To dominate
Not-yet-warming seas.

The White Whale hears—
Stillness and contemplation
From the flounder
Whose eyes scan the flat bottom
In opposite directions.

The White Whale hears—
The screech of the frigate birds
Who gather off the whaleship's bow
Awaiting scraps
And knowing what's to come.

The White Whale hears—
A slowness encroaching,

As the *P.* exits the North Equatorial Current
Standing toward the center of the Gyre
Where plastic reigns today.

The White Whale hears—
The accumulation of unbleached
Corals, building lives upon lives
In clear water, infiltrated
By clownfish and moray eels.

The White Whale hears—
The mouth of the Giant Clam open
Admitting water,
And shut again
After some time.

The White Whale hears—
Voices of tiny men
In the rigging,
Singing work songs
And furling canvas.

The White Whale hears—
Far off in rocky Nantucket,
The voice of a boy,
Whose father is at sea.

The White Whale hears—
The fluid displacement
Of the Blue Whale,
Earth's most massive swimmer
In the deepest seas.

The White Whale hears—
Tashtego the Gay Head Indian

Ascend the main
To take Q.'s place
At the watching.

The White Whale hears—
No pegleg
In no augur hole
No harsh voice
Championing violence.

The White Whale hears—
The soft feet of I.
Sneaking toward the foremast
To climb one last time
In darkness
Before dawn.

The White Whale hears—
So many more things
That not song nor computation
Can number them.

Having heard
So widely that all the universe
Is known,
Moby-Dick swims
            now!
And all undersea creation
Fan-tails in his wake.

The Chase—Third Day

The things that come together do not
Equal each other.

The *P.* floats in glorious confusion,
Bearing Q.'s majesty, Pip's madness, Stubb's boldness,
The queer wisdom of the old Manxman,
The regenerating curiosity of I.,
All floating together,
Not in harmony but in company,
Parceled into whaleboats
Sleeping within one Nantucket keel,
A coffin made of American wood,
Inside a dream of acquisition,
Reaching for oil and sperm,
Grasping—what? Nothing—
At the last?

Opposite the whaleship swims the forehead
Of Moby-Dick, *combinedly possessed* by the strength
Of *all the angels that fell from heaven.*

Oh, Flask, cries the Mate, misquoting Shakespeare—
For one red cherry
Ere we die. Cherries? replies King-Post,
I only wish that we were where they grow.

And the predestinating head
Swims his predestinated path
Across fatal waves
Into God-denying keel
Drowning utopia.
Christians and pagans and carpenters,
Cooks and blacksmiths and mast-mounted Q.,

Manxmen and Lascars and Parsees,
Pip and Flask and Starbuck,
Silent Fedallah and more-silent Bulkington,
Sink,
All sink.

Tashtego's arm, raised highest, sinks last
With the main-truck,
But not before intercepting
The archangelic hawk,
Hammering her wing tight into the flag of conquest,
Dragging down with the *P*.
The sea-bird of heaven
Into the *great shroud*
Of the sea.

Epilogue

I.
I. alone
I. all alone
I. floating
Coffin-buoyed
Inscribed wood
The last caress I. feels
Of Q.'s drowned body.
It supports I.
Sharks bite it not.
Savage sea-hawks
Circle
Do not descend.
I. floats.
I. alone.
Soft sea.
Dirge-like.
I.
I. traces
I. traces the lines
Of tattoos carved
Into the wood.
I. alone.
I. sees
Outside the vital center
Devious-cruising
The *Rachel*
Towards him
Retracing
Resailing
Repatterning pathless waves
In search of

Only finding
I.
I. alone
Another orphan.

A Critical Postscript: Cyborgs, Whalemen, and Other Voyagers in *Moby-Dick*

> They were one man, not thirty. . . . Ahab their one
> lord and keel.
> — The Chase, Second Day (415)[1]

> With the problem of the universe revolving in me,
> how could I . . . but lightly hold my obligations to
> uphold all whaleships' standing orders?
> — The Mast-Head (135)

A hole appears in *Moby-Dick* in the wake that Ahab's monomania plows into the great waters. This postscript aims less to fill that emptiness than to take the measure of the Captain's imagined absence.[2] Taking a cue from the double structure of the novel, as famously diagnosed by Charles Olson in *Call Me Ishmael* (1947), the figures of Ahab and Ishmael can represent two substantially distinct philosophical and literary strategies for characterizing selfhood, material embodiment, and the human relationship with the ocean. These two modes of thinking do not define the voyage so much as metaphorically divide it. Ahab's trajectory is singular, vitalist, and focused on forging multiple cyborg assemblages into a coherent whole. To Ahab the world ocean comprises one vast hunting ground. His composites unfurl through intersections of the humanities and the sciences. Ahab's vision catches theoretical echoes in the writings of modern critics of cyborg identities and human-nonhuman assemblages such as Donna Haraway, Bruno

[A slightly different version of this chapter was first published under the title, "Sailing without Ahab," in *Ahab Unbound: Melville and the Materialist Turn*, ed. Meredith Farmer and Jonathan D. S. Schroeder (Minneapolis: University of Minnesota Press, 2021), 47–64. Reprinted with permission.]

Latour, and Karen Barad. The Captain's cyborgism also takes in much of the dominant critical tradition of reading *Moby-Dick* after Melville's twentieth-century revival, even as twenty-first-century critics are expanding Ahab's identities in new directions.

Charles Olson's theory that *Moby-Dick* emerged from a series of sometimes conflicting drafts suggests the possibility of a second, less well-known Ishmaelite strain in the novel. (Readers of Harrison Hayford's "Unnecessary Duplicates" will have encountered the idea of Melville's doubled narratives, but Olson got there decades earlier.)[3] Ishmael represents plurality against Ahab's monomania. Ishmael is lyrical rather than epic, overlapping rather than distinct, variable rather than unified. The contrast between Ahab's singularity and Ishmael's plurality sits at the center of their symbolic opposition—though Ahab also contains multitudes and Ishmael sometimes rests in solitary reveries. The bow oarsman seeks oceanic truths but sometimes misses whales. He sleeps on the job. His conceptual position resonates with twenty-first-century ecomaterialist feminist theories that explore porosity and exchange within and beyond human bodies, including the works of Rosi Braidotti, Stacy Alaimo, and Lowell Duckert. I call this trend life-buoy ecomaterialism, remembering that in Melville's novel, the last and most important life buoy is the coffin of an Indigenous man, decorated with unintelligible symbols.

The rival strains of Ahab's cyborgism and Ishmael's ecomaterialism intertwine and entangle themselves throughout Melville's novel. On a narrative level, my project of "sailing without Ahab" remains literally impossible. Ahab represents the dominant principle of direction in Melville's oceanic epic. He smashes the quadrant and steers by his own will (377–79). But through an experiment in turning away from the egotistical center it may be possible to glimpse alternate, antityrannical poetics swirling around Melville's novel. The contrast between cyborgism and ecomaterialism also articulates an ethical core that opposes the singular to the plural. Ahab's assemblages forge themselves through manic pressure and control; he creates unity through force. Ishmael, on the other hand, celebrates plural knowledges and ethical acceptances. Taking to his bosom a pagan friend even before embarking on the *Pequod*, Ishmael weaves together the arcane knowledges of nascent ocean-ography, literary and artistic history, religious doctrines, and even the undecipherable tattoos on Queequeg's body. By considering "Ahab" and "Ishmael" as theoretically detachable from the con-ceptual universe of *Moby-Dick*, this Postscript explores both what these figures represent and what options might emerge if the cen-trality of either one were diminished.

In Olson's poetic reading, the essential additions to the first draft of *Moby-Dick* emerged out of Melville's intellectual encoun-ter with Shakespeare. For Olson, the mature tragic vision of *King Lear* and *Macbeth* ballasts *Moby-Dick* with metaphorical grandeur. Olson's critical response to Melville starts by isolating the key item the earliest draft of the novel lacks. "*Moby-Dick*," he writes, "was two books written between February, 1850 and August, 1851. The first book did not contain Ahab."[4] Olson argues that Melville's deepening and expanding the early draft of the sea yarn came about through his encounter with "the ferment, Shakespeare, the cause" (39). Olson discerns the influence of Shakespeare's high tragic mode on the evolving conceptions of the novel. Thus Olson pronounces that the weakly redemptive figure of Albany in *King Lear* "is a Starbuck" (49), while the novel's tormented and supernaturally inflected "Ahab-world" resembles *Macbeth* even more than *King Lear* (53). Olson's conception of the completed *Moby-Dick* remains deeply Ahab-centered because only Ahab presents Shakespeare's high tragic vision of heroism at odds with universal laws. In suggesting that Ahab represents the novel's central conceit and philosophical vision, Olson remains bounded by the Captain's cyborgism. At times, Olson appears to have caught a glimmer of Ishmael's anti-Ahabian musings, and in ways to which I'll return, his concluding vision of "Pacific Man" (114–19) owes some of its distinctive flavor to the novel's Ishma-elite strain. But in focusing on the "god" (82) that he sees Mel-ville presenting in the Captain, Olson leans into Ahabism. Using

Olson as touchstone and point of departure, my Postscript aims to surface Ishmael's plural countermelodies, entwined with and working against Ahabian maximalism. The result will be what Father Mapple calls a "two-stranded lesson" (49) in which both cyborgism and ecomaterialist alternatives become visible.

This Postscript comprises three sections and a poetic conclusion. First, "Ahab's Cyborgism" takes special aim at Melville's chapter named "Ahab" as well as the initial moment of contact with the White Whale on the First Day of the Chase. These moments construct Ahabism as a fantasy of mechanical hybridity hostile to the holistic mysteries of the deep ocean. The second section, "Ishmaelism and Other Fantasies," takes its cue from the narrator sleeping away his watch at the Mast-Head, at which moment he seems blissfully free of Ahab's control. In a literal sense, Ishmael aloft strains as far from his Captain as he can place himself; in symbolic terms, he nearly escapes Ahab's gravity. I juxtapose this philosophical escape with the crisis of corporate identity that befalls the *Pequod* on the Second Day of the Chase, during which Ahab loses his artificial leg and the cyborg life force for which that leg stands. A third section, "Sailing without Ahab," takes up the last day of the Chase and the imaginary pluralities toward which the relationship between Ishmael and Queequeg gestures. A poetic conclusion enlists the shadow-partner Bulkington as incitement to restless and endless voyaging. The cumulative argument suggests that bringing Ishmaelite alternatives in contact with the dominant Ahabian structures of the novel can draw out an oceanic ecopoetics of entanglement and access particularly valuable in our Anthropocene age.

Ahab's Cyborgism

He arrives late, and ominously. It is not until the twenty-fifth chapter that Ishmael describes him on board the *Pequod*: "Reality outran apprehension: Captain Ahab stood upon his quarter-deck" (108). In delaying the Captain's arrival and in carefully signaling his symbolic possession of the southbound *Pequod* ("his quarter-deck"), Melville trains our attention on this singular figure. Ahab represents the backbone of the novel, the driving motivation behind the Chase, and Melville's most resonant creation. But in the chapter that introduces the Captain in command of his vessel, a complex interface between man, prosthetic, and ship takes center stage:

> I was struck with the singular posture he maintained. Upon each side of the *Pequod*'s quarter deck, and pretty close to the mizzen shrouds, there was an auger hole, bored about half an inch or so, into the plank. His bone leg steadied in that hole; one arm elevated, and holding by a shroud; Captain Ahab stood erect, looking straight out beyond the ship's ever-pitching prow. There was an infinity of firmest fortitude, a determinate, unsurrenderable willfulness, in the fixed and fearless, forward dedication of that glance. (109)

The adjectival cascade "firmest . . . determinate . . . fixed and fearless" decorates the Captain and focuses his forward-facing vision. His erect posture, however, requires the combined labor of not just his own body's strength but also a tripartite mechanism: the prosthetic leg, the auger hole, and the shroud on which he leans his elevated arm. While erect posture may be humanity's defining position, especially by contrast with nonhuman beasts (such as legless cetaceans), Ahab's ability to stand is doubly mediated by technology, both his own personal prosthetic and the corporate body of the ship. "Shrouds" refer in sailor talk to the standing rigging fixed from the mast to the deck; these lines are often tarred and do not move during a voyage. In Melville's literary idiom, however, the Captain's supporting shrouds anticipate the "great shroud of the sea" (427) under which the *Pequod*, its Captain, and its crew ultimately sink at the the novel's end. Ahab arrives to the quarterdeck as cyborg assemblage. Among the plural machines that compose and support his body, he bears the shroud of his own final submerging dive.

Beyond the material plurality of Ahab's statue-like deportment lies an emotional horror. In contrast to the visible and symbolic structures of his posture, there appears in his silence and lack of human fellowship what Melville describes as "a crucifixion in his face . . . the nameless regal overbearing dignity of some mighty woe" (109). This foreboding accents Ahab's melodramatic appearance, and while Melville rarely shies away from melodrama, he does hybridize Ahab. When the weather warms as the *Pequod* sails toward the tropics, even "Ahab did, in the end, a little respond to the playful allurings" of warmth in the wind. Ahab's emotional life like his legs remains half human and half mechanical. "More than once," notes Ishmael from his perch on the forenoon watch, "did he put forth the faint blossom of a look, which, in any other man, would have soon flowered out in a smile" (110). No grins show on the Captain's face, because that face does not express the same human identity as "any other man." Spring winds blow, but they find only partial harbors in Ahab.

The cyborg identity that Ahab represents calls up theoretical echoes in the work of late twentieth-century critical thinkers who have attempted to unite the sciences and the humanities, such as Donna Haraway and Bruno Latour. Haraway's celebrated "Cyborg Manifesto," which she describes as "an ironic political myth faithful to feminism, socialism, and materialism," may seem an odd match for Melville's male-dominated sea story.[5] But Haraway's project of blurring "the difference between natural and artificial, mind and body, self-developing and externally designed" (11) enables a reading of Ahab, the pegleg, and the shroud as triply-bodied cyborg composite. Similarly, Bruno Latour's fascination with the agency of nonhuman actors leads him to dispense with the distinction between human and nonhuman: "The human is not a constitutional pole to be opposed to that of the nonhuman."[6] The name of the game for Latour is "morphism," and his proposed term for the human is "weaver of morphisms" (137). In these terms, Ahab as composite figure, equally made up of man and bone-leg and ship, functions as not-only-human morphic agent. Both Haraway, who was trained as a biologist, and Latour, whose home discipline is science studies, use scientific figures and terms such as the cyborg or morphism to bring together the discourses of the arts and the sciences. Perhaps the most radical recent extension of the mutual interpenetrations of these discourses appears in the philosophical writings of Karan Barad, herself trained as a theoretical physicist before embarking on an academic career in critical theory. Barad emphasizes "the constructed nature of scientific knowledge" in ways that parallel both Haraway and Latour, but she also moves beyond these earlier thinkers in advancing a theory of "agential realism" in dialogue with the "philosophy-physics" of Niels Bohr.[7] These critics of material identity suggest that Ahab's multiple corporalities represent an attempt to, in Barad's phrase, "meet the universe"—though Ahab perhaps would hubristically wish to exceed the universe—"halfway." The Captain performs cyborg-as-only-partly-conscious-tyrant, gathering into himself objects external to himself in order to increase his own power and range.

The connection between body-as-unity and external objects that the body attempts to incorporate resurfaces near the novel's end when Ahab claims the doubloon at the start of the Chase. The gold coin, symbol of the quest for Moby-Dick that Ahab himself had nailed to the mast, returns to the Captain in the end. "The doubloon is mine," Ahab cries, gainsaying Tashtego, who also raised the White Whale, "Fate reserved the doubloon for me. _I_ only" (408). The racist implications of having the white Nantucket Captain overrule the Indigenous Gay Head harpooner seem clear. In reincorporating the doubloon at the start of the three-day Chase, Ahab reinforces his cyborg authority by excluding the Indigenous perspective. Ahab pronounces himself the central mystery and truth in his cosmos:

> The firm tower, that is Ahab; the volcano, that is Ahab; the courageous, the undaunted, and victorious fowl, that, too, is Ahab; all are Ahab; and this round gold is but the image of the rounder globe, which, like a magician's glass, to each and every man in turn but mirrors back his own mysterious self. (332)

The Captain contains within himself all agencies: man, pegleg, shroud, and also doubloon. Melville's emphasis on the nonhuman matter that Ahab incorporates into himself contrasts sharply with the divine and living appearance of the White Whale:

> A gentle joyousness—a mighty mildness of repose in swiftness, invested the gliding whale. . . . On each soft side—coincident with that parted swell, that but once leaving him, then flowed so wide away—on each bright side, the whale shed off enticings. (409)

Moby-Dick's mild nature inverts Ahab's violence, but even more precisely the whale's plural unities together with the single parting of the ocean's swell overwrite Ahab's assembled parts. The whale appears at last as the "white bull Jupiter" and "the grand god" (409). The description of Ahab with his whaleboat caught in Moby-Dick's jaws brings the biotic whale and cyborg boat-human assemblage into direct opposition: "the long, narrow, scrolled lower jaw curled high up into the open air, and one of the teeth caught in a row-lock" (410). Ahab grasps the whale's massive jaw with his "naked hands" (410) but ends up rescued in Stubb's boat "like one trodden under foot of herds of elephants" (411). In the conflict between divine body and cyborg assemblage, the human-machine composite proves the weaker.

Ishmaelism and Other Fantasies

Treating Melville's novel as the epic of Ahab remains standard practice among critics and in classrooms. Olson, despite his interest in the novel's dual form, reads Ishmael as "a chorus through whom Ahab's tragedy is seen" (57). In evocative but brief comments on the novel's narrator, however, Olson observes that Ishmael perceives things invisible to the Captain. Ishmael "alone hears Father Mapple's sermon out. He alone saw Bulkington . . . [and he alone] learned the secrets of Ahab's blasphemies from the prophet of the fog, Elijah" (58). Turning critical attention from Ahab's dictatorial control to Ishmael's wandering philosophy splinters cyborgism into plural and posthuman seas. Ishmael occupies the center of attention by himself only at the end of the Chase, when he floats peacefully on the coffin life-buoy provided by Queequeg as the *Pequod* descends into the maelstrom. In Ishmael's intermittent vision, however, the novel's conception of humanity's relation to oceanic nature becomes less conflict obsessed and more speculative. Selfhood becomes distributed and plural. Across the posthuman divide lies Ishmael's dreamy Pantheism and indifference to the Chase.

Ishmael rejects Ahab's drive for sovereignty, and it is through the bow oarsman's refusal that Melville's oceanic connections to posthuman ecofeminism seem most clear. Stacy Alaimo's recent volume, *Exposed* (2016), emphasizes that dethroning the supreme individual's heroic conflict with nature epitomizes her ecomaterialist approach. "I would like to recast," she writes, "loss of sovereignty . . . as an invitation to intersubjectivity or trans-subjectivity and even . . . to a posthumanist sense of the self as opening out unto the larger material world and being penetrated by all sorts of substances and material agencies."[8] Writing in the tradition of Rosi Braidotti's "life beyond the self," Alaimo leverages the ecofeminist materialist position to emphasize the mutual porosity of human bodies, nonhuman entities, and other materials.[9] Like Ishmael, and also like other scholars in the emerging ecodiscourse of the blue humanities, Alaimo finds inspiration in the complex materiality of the ocean.[10] The great salt sea presses on human minds and bodies, showing their borders to be less than solid or fixed. Melville's combination of obsessive maritime particularity and Ishmael's theorizing tendencies both recall elements of blue humanities scholarship about human bodies and the ocean. Elspeth Probyn's exploration of the "cultural politics of more-than-human marine entanglement" takes her into critical and ecological theory and also into the material abundance of the Sydney fish market.[11] In a more literary context, Lowell Duckert finds that engaging with water generates "epistemological uncertainty and endless interlocutions."[12] Ishmael's hydro-fascination, announced in the opening "Loomings" chapter via the claim that "meditation and water are wedded for ever" (19), finds intellectual kinship in these speculative oceanic ecotheorists. In ocean-loving Ishmael, Melville produces a literary precursor for the recent turn toward the sea in the blue ecohumanities.

Ishmael's diffuse presence permeates *Moby-Dick*, and a full survey of the way his anti-Ahabian rhetoric suffuses and shapes the novel would require more space than is available here. The apex symbol of Ishmael's anti-Ahabian nature comes in chapter 35, "The Mast-Head." When Ishmael ascends to the highest point on the *Pequod*, in that airy reverie he escapes his Captain's rhythm and even the confines of his schoolmaster's grammar: "In the serene weather of the tropics it is exceedingly pleasant—the mast-head, nay, to a dreamy meditative man it is delightful. . . . [E]verything resolves you into languor" (133).[13] The ascent into "languor" represents a brief respite from narrative itself. Nothing happens while Ishmael keeps watch. While aloft, Ismael philosophizes but does not labor. He values the "sublime uneventfulness" (133) that raising a whale would shatter. "Ye ship-owners of Nantucket!" he warns, "beware of enlisting in your vigilant fisheries any lad with lean brow and hollow eye, given to unreasonable meditativeness" (135). Ishmael sees nothing from the mast-head: no whales, no cries, no forward movement in the epic of the White Whale. Ishmael's ascent makes visible an antinarrative thread in the novel that entwines itself around and arguably delays Ahab's mad forward thrusting. In considering the full sweep of *Moby-Dick*'s 135 chapters, the division between clearly narrative and action-based episodes (i.e., The Chase, Stubb Kills a Whale, The Doubloon) and more reflective or pedagogical episodes (i.e., The Whiteness of the Whale, The Sperm Whale's Head, Cetology) appears hard to parse, though it seems likely that the division is not far from even.[14] Ishmael asleep at the mast-head fixes un-narrating at its literal top, though in the slow roll of ship on the sea Melville finds the lurking possibility of a brief and violent interruption:

But while this sleep, this dream, is on ye, move your foot or hand an inch, slip your hold at all, and your identity comes back in horror. Over Descartian vortices you hover. And perhaps, at mid-day, in the fairest weather, with one half-throttled shriek you drop through that transparent air into the summer sea, no more to rise for ever. (136)

From non-narrative dreaming into sudden deadly drama, the philosopher at least hypothetically falls. The posthumanist philosophies of Alaimo and Duckert might characterize the fall into the sea in terms of entanglement and transcorporality, but that leaves our narrator's voice no less silenced.

In mid-reverie Ishmael appears as free from Ahab's command as he ever can be, but the forward press of the novel's plot subjects him repeatedly to his Captain's will. On the Second Day of the Chase, Ishmael's subjection shows itself as he describes the whale-boats striking out for Moby-Dick through a sustained metaphor of incorporation: "They were one man, not thirty" (415). In this instant, all the whalemen, including Ishmael, become ship-cy-borgs like their Captain: "For as the one ship that held them all . . . [contained] one concrete hull, which shot on its way, both balanced and directed by the long central keel, even so . . . all varieties were welded into oneness, and were all directed to that fatal goal which Ahab their lord and keel did point to" (415). The men are doubly constructed as cyborgs, in that they have become analogous to the structure of the *Pequod* and that they follow Ahab as both divine "lord" and mechanical "keel." Fully melded into an identity composed of their Captain's will and the tools of their violent trade, the whalemen seek Moby-Dick, find him, and in the ensuing melee lose both Ahab's artificial leg and Starbuck's goodwill. The symbolic focus of the Second Day, like that of The Chase in all three of its parts, submerges Ishmael's plurality. The narrator's name does not appear in any of these three chapters. The lust of the hunt displaces the meditative freedom glimpsed from the mast-head.

When Ahab's leg breaks on the Second Day, his cyborg assem-blage fractures and he briefly becomes dependent. Starbuck, who wishes that "old Ahab had leaned oftener than he has" (417), might be proposing a human and collective identity, opposed to Ahab's monolithic structure of human and mechanical solitary command. Starbuck occupies a human middle space, not a cyborg like his Captain, but also not the fully anti-Ahabian self-lessness of Ishmael. Seminarrative chapters such as "A Squeeze of the Hand," which work with sperm oil but do not drive the crew into a violent frenzy, may also display anti-Ahabian collective possibilities that are distinct from Ishmael's forays into selfless solitude. In rejecting Starbuck's plea, "In Jesus' name no more of this" (418), Ahab deifies himself as cyborg composite: "Ahab is for ever Ahab, man. This whole act's immutably decreed. 'Twas rehearsed by thee and me a billion years before this ocean rolled" (418). Celebrating himself as "the Fates' lieutenant" (418), Ahab rejects Starbuck's religious understanding of community and also Ishmael's anti-individualist undersong. The carpenter fashions the Captain's new leg from "the broken keel of Ahab's wrecked craft" (419), indicating both that the new cyborg will continue to function as keel and backbone of his crew and that the fantasy of unity he represents has itself been broken.

Sailing without Ahab

If not Ahab, then who? Ishmael and Ahab exchange no direct words in the novel, though as a crewmember Ishmael self-names his inclusion, that "I, Ishmael, was one of that crew" (152), at the quarter-deck swearing on the doubloon to hunt Moby-Dick. Alternative communities abound in the novel, including Fedallah and his Parsee oarsmen, the distinct groups of mates and harpooners, and the particular visionary case of Pip. But the closest alternative pole to Ahab must be Queequeg the Indigenous South Seas harpooner, Ishmael's bosom friend and shipmate. If Ishmael represents a metaphysical loss of self and communion with the vast sea, and Ahab a hypertrophied ego and rage against nonhuman beasts, Queequeg suggests the possibility of perfected and polytheistic humanity. As "George Washington cannibalistically developed" (55), he combines a physical ideal with expansive moral reach. "I'll try a pagan friend," muses Ishmael, "since Christian kindness has proved but hollow" (56). Queequeg's friendship amounts to an idealized homoerotic marriage of emotional community, "a cosy, loving pair" (57) as Ishmael calls the two of them on their second night together at the Spouter-Inn. The queer multiracial union miniaturizes and idealizes the polyglot *Pequod*—though Ishmael and Queequeg appear in the novel prior to, and to some extent independently of, Ahab's doomed quest. The Ishmael and Queequeg love story forms its own anti-Ahabian counterplot, in some ways more potent than Ishmael's musings in moments of solitude.

Following Olson's split image of the composition of *Moby-Dick*, it is possible to imagine an alternative book focused on Queequeg, which might have followed the Polynesian template that produced Melville's previous commercial successes in *Typee* and *Omoo*. The intrusion of Ahab's darker, and in Olson's reading Shakespearean, tone would have displaced the presumptive South Seas idyll. But unlike some traces of a proto-*Moby-Dick* that appear early in the novel and then vanish, Queequeg keeps his central place in the tragic story. His made-to-order coffin, from which bed he unexpectedly recovers his own life, becomes Ishmael's life-buoy.

Another composite image of the couple appears when Queequeg fixes the blubber hook onto the whale's back while its other end is wrapped around Ishmael's waist onboard the ship in "The Monkey-Rope." Roped together, the pair reprises the language of duality from their prevoyage nights at the Inn. We "were wedded," says Ishmael, by means of an "elongated Siamese ligature" (255). In language that recalls his loss of self in the reverie on the mast-head, Ishmael philosophizes that "my own individuality was now merged in a joint stock company of two" (255). This passage emphasizes that for Ishmael egotism of the Ahabian variety represents death, but selflessness in various form gives life. (Here it may be noteworthy that the monkey-rope is entirely Melville's fiction, not a historical practice of Nantucket whalemen.) Ishmael sees in the vision of Queequeg on the whale's back, surrounded by the dangerous spades of his fellow harpooners, a pretty allegory:

> That unsounded ocean you gasp in, is Life; those sharks, your foes; those spades, your friends; and what between sharks and spades you are in a sad pickle and peril, poor lad. (256)

Wanting to interpret the labor of whaling as symbolic code for nineteenth-century American life was an occupational hazard for Melville—as, perhaps, reading whaling as a representation of the environmental destruction that follows extractive oil-seeking industries is for twenty-first-century Melvillian ecocritics.[15] What seems striking about the image of the monkey-rope is the dualist middle alternative it poses between Ahab's singularity and Ishmael's dissolution. Ishmael becomes finally singular at the novel's end, since Queequeg goes down with the *Pequod*—but earlier in the novel the savage harpooner represents the tantalizing possibility of sailing without Ahab and yet not alone.

Even with Queequeg as a possible middle option, the trajectory of *Moby-Dick* forces the binary choice between Ahab and Ishmael. Most readers, and most critics, very much including Olson, have cast their lots with the Captain. Oscillating between mast-head Pantheism and monkey-rope fatalism, Ishmael articulates an in-between position that echoes the boundary-crossing arguments advanced by contemporary ecomaterialist critics from Alaimo to Duckert. In one recent essay, Alaimo reads the dissolving shells of sea creatures as an analogy for radical and painful openness to ecological change: "This is a call for scale shifting that is intrepidly—even psychedelically—empathetic, rather than safely ensconced. Contemplating your shell on acid dissolves individualist, consumerist subjectivity" (168). In Alaimo's reading, the dissolving shell resembles drowsy Ishmael aloft. Duckert, in a comparable vein but with a slightly different material focus, asks that readers imagine themselves into sympathy with glaciers, swamps, and other unfriendly forms of water, "not to make clear the muddy waters of reality, but to delve deeper into their turbulent flows" (42). Sailing without Ahab but with Ishmael entertains these extreme and uncomfortable ecological entanglements. No direction but outward, into alien vastness: like a sleeping lookout precariously balanced in the rigging, the Ahab-less sailor lacks purpose, drive, even motion. Some contemporary ecotheorists wager that this unstructured experience of the nonhuman can lead to a deeper and perhaps more real connection to the world beyond ourselves.

Bulkington at Sea

"Wonderfullest things are ever the unmentionable," says Ishmael, introducing the "six-inch chapter" that is the "stoneless grave of Bulkington" (96). This mostly offstage Virginian mariner previously described as the novel's "sleeping-partner" (29) provides one final alternative guide into the "wonder-world" (22) of the *Pequod*'s voyage. Bulkington looks the hero's part: "full six feet in height, with noble shoulders, and a chest like a coffer-dam" (29). A southerner who appeared to Ishmael like "one of those tall mountaineers from the Alleghanian Ridge in Virginia" (29), Bulkington appears at first to represent a regional alternative to the northeastern fallen Dutch aristocracy that roughly defines Ishmael's (and Melville's) cultural roots. If so, the narrator's relationship to the sailor he calls "my comrade" (29) may represent an American alliance that might span the growing North-South divide of the 1840s. Bulkington's vision, like Ishmael's, and perhaps also like Queequeg's, the only other shipmate termed "comrade," is oceanic rather than terrestrial: "in landlessness alone resides the highest truth, shoreless indefinite as God" (97). In Bulkington's barest touching of land—a few nights ashore after a four years' voyage before launching again with the *Pequod*—Melville constructs an organizing principle based on nonhuman sea rather than familiar land.

For Olson, Bulkington's heroic shape represents "right reason" (Olson, 57), which stares directly into tragedy with open eyes. In this reading, "he is the crew's heart, the sign of their paternity, the human thing" (57). By contrast, Ishmael stands somewhat apart from the hero and the "apotheosis" (57) that Olson sees in the *Pequod*'s loss. Olson draws the term "apotheosis" directly from Melville's last word of Bulkington's chapter, but interestingly he does not quote the passage in full. "Take heart, take heart, O Bulkington!" rhapsodizes Ishmael. "Bear thee grimly, demigod! Up from the spray of thy ocean-perishing—straight up, leaps thy apotheosis!" (Melville, 97). This passage assimilates human hero into godlike whale, whose breaching "into the pure element of the air" on the Second Day of the Chase "is his act of defiance" (415). Unlike Ishmael, Olson seems not to connect Bulkington's "landlessness" directly to Moby-Dick. Melville implies that both whale and silent sailor entirely reject landed life. If sailing with Queequeg might conceivably represent a cozy coffin-boat built for two, taking advantage of the secret knowledge of Indigenous Pacific Islanders, sailing with Bulkington rejects all comforts: his ship "must fly all hospitality, one touch of land, though it but graze the keel, would make her shudder through and through" (Olson, 97). Both of Ishmael's comrades represent turns away from Ahabian monomania, but Bulkington steers more directly into inhuman death and depths.

While Ishmael occupies the squishy center of an anti-Ahabian reading of *Moby-Dick*, Bulkington defines a pure oceanic radicalism. As sailor he transforms his American heroic visage into something that resembles a marine creature. Queequeg, who hails from the imaginary island of "Kokovoko" (59), presents a queer multiracial utopian fantasy that saves Ishmael's life via the coffin life-buoy. It may also be possible to read Ishmael less optimistically as a kind of colonizer, using Queequeg's coffin to safe his own life after the Indigenous hero has drowned. (This reading recalls James Fenimore Cooper's paradigm, in which the dying Indigenous sage passes his wisdom down to a worthy white man.) But whether lovers or colonial partners, Ishmael and Queequeg at least hint at a humanized version of whaling. Bulkington by contrast captures the tragic impossibility of expanding human experience into the fullness of oceanic space.

Trying to come to grips with these fantasies within the world of *Moby-Dick* was one of the first puzzles to lead me beyond traditional literary criticism into ecopoetry. One of the first-written poems of *Sailing without Ahab* sought via Bulkington's chapter, "The Lee Shore," a rejection of human society that both echoes and displaces Ahab's solitude. In Bulkington's turn away from the noisy Spouter-Inn toward his voyage on the *Pequod*, I imagine a turn away from human society that returns to sea in complete ignorance of Ahab's quest. Bulkington must be included in the "one man not thirty" who row toward the White Whale on the Second Day, but Melville's submersion of this enigmatic figure throughout the voyage allows us to imagine him as sailing almost independently, largely free from the tyrant's command. In my reading, Bulkington chooses "landlessness" because he eschews humanity:

Bulkington's Out

There's a pause just at journey's end—
a still point, landfall, feet touching ground.
Voices and noises surround you.
An unsettling place, footfall.
People looking a certain way.
Shipfall: still floating?
In darkness the dock buzzes possibility.
Why stay?[16]

Being enclosed by people and their "certain" looks in the Spouter-Inn, Bulkington unsettles. He refuses stillness, even the brief pause through which his walking feet touch solid ground. The ship's floating landlessness calls him, though the distracting people at this point are in the Spouter-Inn in New Bedford while the *Pequod* floats off Nantucket. "Why stay?" catechizes the wisdom of anti-Ahabs like Bulkington, Queequeg, and Ishmael. Against singularity the question, "Why stay?," poses options. Against stasis it proffers movement. Against certainty it opens into the interrogative. It is neither route finder nor strategy but an openness to change and dissolution. Whatever its names, it remains suspicious of the self.

Sailing without Ahab in this plural concept recasts some of the outward-bound visions of "Pacific Man" with which Olson concludes *Call Me Ishmael* (114–19). The Pacific for Olson is the American "HEART SEA . . . the Plains repeated" (114), but it's worth recalling that when the *Pequod* first enters Pacific waters, that ocean carries the special mark not of Ahab but Ishmael, who describes "my dear Pacific" (367) with intimate enthusiasm: "this mysterious, divine Pacific zones the world's whole bulk about; makes all coasts one bay to it; seems the tide-beating heart of earth. Lifted by those eternal swells, you needs must own the seductive god, bowing your head to Pan" (367). Olson may ultimately claim the last American voyage west into the Pacific Ocean as the "third and final Odyssey [that] was Ahab's" (118)—but the novel suggests that this oceanic encounter connects instead to Ishmael's pantheistic reverie.[17]

Focusing on Ishmael puts Melville's maritime epic in touch with twenty-first-century ecotheoretical modes that reject traditional values of individuality and coherence. It seems risky to transform the most canonical American novel of the nineteenth century into anachronistic ecomaterialist modes. I would not claim that Melville, or many of Melville's readers, would want or value an Ahab-less novel. But as the twenty-first century tallies up the cost of sailing under the flags of questing heroes and oil-seeking industries, it's helpful to find in one of our literature's ur-texts an alternative. Ishmaelism may not represent a path, or even a fully coherent direction, but its counter-song within *Moby-Dick* connects to new ways ecotheorists and humanities scholars are describing the human-environment relationship in our warming present. Perhaps the polyglot *Pequod*, with its multiracial queer crew, can shake off the controlling hand of her one-legged master and sail into plural oceans, whether whales are to be found or not.

Notes

A slightly different version of this chapter was first published under the title "Sailing without Ahab" in *Ahab Unbound: Melville and the Materialist Turn*, ed. Meredith Farmer and Jonathan D. S. Schroeder (Minneapolis: University of Minnesota Press, 2021), 47–64. Reprinted with permission.

1. Herman Melville, *Moby-Dick*, ed. Hershel Parker and Harrison Hayford (New York: Norton, 2002), 415. All further citations from *Moby-Dick* given in the text by page number.

2. The poetic project of this book comprises a slightly different attempt to "fill" Ahab's imagined emptiness. The first installation of the project appeared in the *Glasgow Review of Books* in April 2017: *https://glasgowreviewofbooks.com/2017/04/11/sailing-without-ahab-an-eco-poetic-voyage/.* Accessed 2 August 2018.

3. Harrison Hayford, "Unnecessary Duplicates: A Key to the Writing of *Moby-Dick*," in *Moby-Dick* (New York: Norton, 2002), 674-96.

4. Charles Olson, *Call Me Ishmael* (New York: Grove Press, 1947), 35. Further citations in the text.

5. Donna Haraway, "The Cyborg Manifesto" (1984), in *Manifestly Haraway* (Minneapolis: University of Minnesota Press, 2016), 5. Further citations in the text.

6. Bruno Latour, *We Have Never Been Modern*, trans. Catherine Porter (Cambridge, MA: Harvard University Press, 1993), 137.

7. Karan Barad, *Meeting the Universe Halfway: Quantum Physics and the Entanglement of Matter and Meaning* (Durham, NC: Duke University Press, 2007), 39, 69.

8. Stacy Alaimo, *Exposed: Environmental Politics and Pleasures in Posthuman Times* (Minneapolis: University of Minnesota Press, 2016), 4.

9. Rosi Braidotti, *The Posthuman* (Cambridge: Polity Press, 2013), 13–54.

10. On the oceanic turn in the humanities, see John Gillis, "The Blue Humanities," *Humanities* 34.3 (2013), *https://www.neh.gov/humanities/2013/mayjune/feature/the-blue-humanities.* Accessed 7 August 2018.

11. Elspeth Probyn, *Eating the Ocean* (Durham, NC: Duke University Press, 2016), 48, 159–63.

12. Lowell Duckert, *For All Waters: Finding Ourselves in Early Modern Wetscapes* (Minneapolis: University of Minnesota Press, 2017), xvi–xvii.

13. For a creative reappropriation of this chapter, see Steve Mentz, "Philosopher at the Masthead," *Shipwreck Modernity: Ecologies of Globalization, 1550–1719* (Minneapolis: University of Minnesota Press, 2017), 129–30.

14. A full accounting would need to determine how to categorize chapters that introduce future actors but do not show them in action yet ("Knights and Squires"), chapters that describe action away from the *Pequod* (the stories of the *Town-Ho*, the *Rose Bud*, etc.), and others that combine a sliver of action with an excess of philosophy ("The Mast-Head," "The

Monkey-Rope"). In lieu of such an arbitrary exercise, I posit that the novel self-consciously divides itself between narrative propulsion and speculative reflection. The contrasting entanglement of these two modes echoes the contrast between Ahab and Ishmael.

15. For a foundational ecocritical reading of Melville, see Lawrence Buell, *The Environmental Imagination: Thoreau, Nature Writing, and the Formation of American Culture* (Cambridge, MA: Harvard University Press, 1996). See also T. Hugh Crawford, "Networking the (Non) Human: *Moby-Dick*, Matthew Fontaine Maury, and Bruno Latour," *Configurations* 5.1 (1997): 1–21; and Phillip Armstrong, "Leviathan Is a Skein of Networks: Translations of Nature and Culture in *Moby-Dick*," *ELH* 71.4 (2004): 1039–63.

16. First published in *Glasgow Review of Books* in "Sailing without Ahab: An Eco-Poetic Voyage," on 11 April 2017: *https://glasgowreviewof-books.com/2017/04/11/sailing-without-ahab-an-eco-poetic-voyage/*. Accessed 8 August 2018.

17. Olson's three Odysseys are Homer's in the Mediterranean, Dante's in the Atlantic, and Ahab's in the Pacific (117–19). But Olson also concludes his book by writing that "the three great creations of Melville and *Moby-Dick* are Ahab, The Pacific, and the White Whale" (119). In my terms, I suggest that what Olson calls "Pacific" might be more clearly named "Ishmael."

Acknowledgments

Many hands have supported this voyage. I'm grateful to my twin Muses: a twenty-year-old coming-apart Norton Critical Edition of *Moby-Dick* that has haunted my steps on years of adventures; and the lands and waters of Short Beach, Connecticut, where I live and swim. To my fellow Short Beachers, human and canine, avian and aquatic, seaweed and jellyfish, I owe daily inspiration. I value the past, ongoing, and future stewardship of Indigenous peoples and nations, especially the Totoket and Menunkatuck bands of the Quinnipiac people, whose presence endures among these lands and waters.

As I have turned toward poetry in recent years, including an urgent intensification during the pandemic, I have received inspiration and support from poets near and far, including my St. John's colleagues Lee Ann Brown, Scott Combs, Greg Maertz, Dan Dissinger, Erik Fuhrer, Peter Vanderberg, Sasha Chinnaya, Stephen Paul Miller, and many others. I owe a debt for inspiration and suggestion to the poets who assembled the glorious collaborative poem-a-day Sonnet Corona Project, especially Shannon Garner, Maureen Daniels, and Art Zilleruelo. For encouragement when I might have stalled, I appreciate my March 2020 cluster of Object Lessons authors, especially Dinah Lenney (*Coffee*) and Erik Anderson (*Bird*), neither of whom I've yet managed to meet outside Zoomtopia. Encouragement for early stabs at the project in 2015 came from Patrick Mahon, the BABEL crew in Toronto, and Idalea Cinquemani at St. John's. A final decisive push came in a fall 2022 workshop at the Rachel Carson Center in Munich; I particularly would like to single out the insights of Nakul Heroor and Teja Šosteric, as well as the imaginative energy of the RCC community.

I am grateful to Meredith Farmer and Jonathan D. S. Schroeder, editors of the volume, *Ahab Unbound: Melville and the Materialist Turn* (Minneapolis: University of Minnesota Press,

2022), for including me on their scholarly voyage. An early version of the poem "The Lee Shore" appeared in their collection.

The expansive universe of creative responders to *Moby-Dick*, from Philip Hoare's brilliant books, inspiring twitter feed, and wizardly curation of the *Big Read* audio version of the novel to Suzanne Conklin Akbari and Chris Piuma's Spouter-Inn podcast, Matt Kish's wonderfully manic *Moby-Dick in Pictures: One Drawing for Every Page*, Elizabeth Schultz and Kylan Rice's *After Moby-Dick: An Anthology of New Poetry*, and many others, have provided hope along the way.

The readers of the manuscript for Fordham University Press, Craig Santos Perez, Josiah Blackmore, and an individual who remains anonymous, have each greatly improved this book, the remaining inadequacies of which remain wholly my own. I value the editorial commitment, insight, and vision of Richard Morrison, whose belief in this project and in the creative mission of scholarly publishing heartens me.

Tom White and the editors of the *Glasgow Review of Books* published two early excerpts from this project, in April 2017 and May 2018. The *Review* published earlier versions of the poems now titled, "Sailing Without," "Loomings," "The Lee Shore," "Glass Foot," and "Great White Evil God."

The map was created for this book by John Wyatt Greenlee of Surprised Eel Mapping.

The two images in the foreword are of the ceramic artwork "Contact, 2021," by Courtney Leonard. Images used by permission of the artist.

I dedicate this book to my parents. My father has been my fishing companion across many decades, and my mother was almost certainly the person who first pressed a copy of *Moby-Dick* into my childish hands.